WHY PHILOSOPHY MATTERS FOR THE STUDY OF RELIGION—AND VICE VERSA

Why Philosophy Matters for the Study of Religion— and Vice Versa

THOMAS A. LEWIS

OXFORD
UNIVERSITY PRESS

OXFORD
UNIVERSITY PRESS

Great Clarendon Street, Oxford, OX2 6DP,
United Kingdom

Oxford University Press is a department of the University of Oxford.
It furthers the University's objective of excellence in research, scholarship,
and education by publishing worldwide. Oxford is a registered trade mark of
Oxford University Press in the UK and in certain other countries

© Thomas A. Lewis 2015

The moral rights of the author have been asserted

First published 2015
First published in paperback 2017

Published in the United States of America by Oxford University Press
198 Madison Avenue, New York, NY 10016, United States of America

British Library Cataloguing in Publication Data

Data available

Library of Congress Cataloging in Publication Data

Data available

ISBN 978-0-19-874474-0 (Hbk.)
ISBN 978-0-19-878525-5 (Pbk.)

For my mother
for inspiration, wisdom, and love

Acknowledgments

The economy of intellectual work is peculiar in many respects. Among others, as we move through time and projects we accumulate more and more debts, without any chance of repaying them. Our best hope is to partially balance them with contributions to others.

This project developed through conversations over years in a variety of settings. Several people convinced me of the need for a vision of philosophy of religion that moves beyond the field's current framing in order to belong more clearly in religious studies. Robert Orsi and Matthew Bagger are among the most important. I am tremendously grateful for their challenges, insight, collegiality, and generosity.

I continue to learn from my former colleagues at Harvard University, particularly Amy Hollywood, David Lamberth, Anne Monius, Parimal Patil, and Ron Thiemann. I daily realize more and more that I learned from Ron; he is sorely missed.

At Brown University, Mark Cladis and Stephen Bush have been better colleagues than one could hope for as I wrote this book. They read early drafts, pushed me for greater clarity, supported the project, and inspired me with their excellence. More recently, Andre Willis and Paul Nahme have added richly to this community. Conversations with Bonnie Honig were invaluable in determining the final form of the project. Nathaniel Berman, Nancy Khalek, Sharon Krause, Elayne Oliphant, Hal Roth, and Michael Steinberg have provided intellectual nourishment and encouragement to think broadly.

Beyond Brown, I have benefited tremendously from conversations with Diana Cates, David Clairmont, Andrew Dole, Eric Gregory, Jennifer Herdt, Grace Kao, John Kelsay, Irene Oh, Wayne Proudfoot, Tyler Roberts, and Kevin Schilbrack. Jeffrey Stout continues to be a model of clarity, precision, and wisdom. Aaron Stalnaker, Elizabeth Bucar, and Jonathan Schofer have been crucial interlocutors, on religious ethics and so much else.

John P. Reeder, Jr. remains in a league of his own. He continues to read and offer penetrating feedback on virtually everything I write. He redefines supererogation in a senior thesis advisor; and that is only the tip of the iceberg of his counsel and friendship.

A number of people generously read part or all of the manuscript and offered tremendous advice. In addition to those mentioned above, I want particularly to thank Kathryn Lofton, Charles Mathewes, Leigh Eric Schmidt, and the anonymous readers from Oxford University Press. The book has benefited substantially from their feedback, even though I have not done justice to their insights.

To my students I owe far more. I am particularly appreciative of Anna "Fannie" Bialek, Niki Clements, Wesley Erdelack, Molly Farneth, Nicholas Friesner, Alexis Glenn, Caroline Kory, David Le, Charles Lockwood, Megan McBride, and Jonathan Sozek. Ben Marcus has been a vital conversation partner in my thinking about religious literacy.

A version of Chapter 1 was presented at the Philosophy of Religions Workshop at the University of Chicago. I am indebted to Dan Arnold, Ryan Coyne, Sarah Hammerschlag, Kevin Hector, and others for their suggestions during that visit as well as in other meetings.

Chapter 2 is a slightly revised version of "On the Role of Normativity in Religious Studies," which originally appeared in *The Cambridge Companion to Religious Studies*, edited by Robert A. Orsi and published by Cambridge University Press (2012). It is reprinted here with permission from Cambridge University Press.

Several conferences at Boston University's Institute for Philosophy and Religion were important for Chapter 3 as well as for the project more generally. I am grateful to David Eckel and Allen Speight for conceiving these events and to them as well as the other participants for so many thought-provoking comments.

A fellowship from the Cogut Center for the Humanities at Brown University provided me with a course release that enabled me to make substantial progress. Both the Cogut Seminar and the Religion and Critical Thought Colloquium participants provided excellent feedback on Chapter 4.

For their insight, patience, and effectiveness, Tom Perridge and Karen Raith at Oxford University Press deserve special thanks.

Finally, Nikki has been a model of persistence, clarity, and innovation—as well as the source of the best kinds of hard questions and love at the same time. And for perspective and patience, Lola and Isobel take the prize.

Contents

Introduction

Mind the Gap: Or, Philosophy of Religion and Religious Studies

When I was an undergraduate in the late 1980s and a graduate student in the early 1990s, method and theory courses seemed to belong to us—those working in philosophy of religion and religious ethics. The readings, themes, and modes of analysis dominant in required seminars on methods and theories were largely philosophical: those of us in these subfields felt we were on home turf, while students specializing in more historical material were often extending themselves to engage in a required exercise far from their central areas of expertise or interest. To use the polemical language of one professor I had, method and theory was the domain of the "thinkers," not the "historians."

Since that time, the ground has shifted. In the last two decades, many of the most significant methodological developments in religious studies have come from those who would have been classed as "historians." The "cultural turn in late ancient studies" as well as the prominence of attention to "lived religion" in American religious history are two obvious examples, though similar developments have taken place in a range of other subfields.[1] This is not to say

---

[1] See, for instance, Dale B. Martin and Patricia Cox Miller, eds., *The Cultural Turn in Late Ancient Studies: Gender, Asceticism, and Historiography* (Durham: Duke University Press, 2005) and David D. Hall, ed., *Lived Religion in America: Toward a History of Practice* (Princeton: Princeton University Press, 1997). For prominent examples from another subfield, see Gregory Schopen, *Bones, Stones, and Buddhist Monks: Collected Papers on the Archaeology, Epigraphy, and Texts of Monastic Buddhism in India* (Honolulu: University of Hawai'i Press, 1997) and Gregory

that such developments were unphilosophical or untheoretical. To the contrary, they were driven largely by greater engagement with theoretical materials by those historians, though they were not by any means passive recipients of theoretical material coming from elsewhere. The result has been that a great deal of historical work has become more theoretically sophisticated and a great deal of theory floats less free of history.

Integral to many of these developments has been a focus on power, practices, and/or material culture. These theoretical developments are diverse, sometimes overlapping but by no means homogeneous. Amidst these developments, an extraordinarily influential body of recent work has interrogated the historical processes through which "religion" has been conceptualized, particularly in the modern West. Studies such as Talal Asad's *Genealogies of Religion* and *Formations of the Secular*, Daniel Dubuisson's *The Western Construction of Religion*, and Tomoko Masuzawa's *The Invention of World Religions*, to mention only a few examples, have frequently attended to the political contexts and consequences of these processes.[2] Their studies have

Schopen, *Buddhist Monks and Business Matters: Still More Papers on Monastic Buddhism in India* (Honolulu: University of Hawai'i Press, 2004).

[2] Talal Asad, *Genealogies of Religion: Discipline and Reasons of Power in Christianity and Islam* (Baltimore: Johns Hopkins University Press, 1993); Talal Asad, *Formations of the Secular: Christianity, Islam, Modernity* (Stanford: Stanford University Press, 2003); Daniel Dubuisson, *The Western Construction of Religion: Myths, Knowledge, and Ideology*, trans. William Sayers (Baltimore: Johns Hopkins University Press, 2003); and Tomoko Masuzawa, *The Invention of World Religions, Or, How European Universalism Was Preserved in the Language of Pluralism* (Chicago: University of Chicago Press, 2005). For other important contributions to this discussion, see Jonathan Z. Smith, *Drudgery Divine: On the Comparison of Early Christianities and the Religions of Late Antiquity* (Chicago: University of Chicago Press, 1990); Jonathan Z. Smith, *Relating Religion: Essays in the Study of Religion* (Chicago: University of Chicago Press, 2004); Hans G. Kippenberg, *Discovering Religious History in the Modern Age*, trans. Barbara Harshav (Princeton: Princeton University Press, 2002); Timothy Fitzgerald, *Discourse on Civility and Barbarity: A Critical History of Religion and Related Categories* (Oxford: Oxford University Press, 2007); David Chidester, *Savage Systems: Colonialism and Comparative Religion in Southern Africa* (Charlottesville: University Press of Virginia, 1996). I have also discussed these developments in Thomas A. Lewis, *Religion, Modernity, and Politics in Hegel* (Oxford: Oxford University Press, 2011), 3–7. The emphasis on practices as well as material culture has fed what many describe as a "new materialism" in religious studies, a cluster of approaches to studying religion that move radically away from attention to belief; see Mark C. Taylor, ed., *Critical Terms for Religious Studies* (Chicago: University of Chicago Press, 1998), and Manuel A. Vásquez, *More than Belief: A Materialist Theory of Religion* (Oxford: Oxford University Press, 2011).

analyzed the central roles attributed to faith and/or belief in many Western accounts of religion, not simply by participants in particular traditions but also in the formation of the academic study of religion. They have highlighted the ways in which this focus on belief and faith has marginalized concerns with practices and objects—whether conceived in terms of rituals, spiritual exercises, disciplines of subject formation, or material culture. For many, this focus on belief and faith derives at least in large part from the Protestant Reformation's emphasis on faith. It is thus deeply interwoven with anti-Catholic polemics in which many ritual practices are deemed mere superstition rather than religion. And this same polemic was frequently deployed in colonial contexts when Europeans encountered native practices. In many cases, the point is not simply a matter of an overemphasis that can be easily corrected; to the contrary, in Asad's judgment, for instance, the category of religion itself is so deeply imbricated in these histories of power and domination that it cannot be effectively recuperated as an analytical concept or category. While some resist this final step in Asad's argument (and argue for the self-conscious use of the category "religion") and debates over subjectivity and subject formation have by no means been settled, this body of material has indelibly marked the broader field of religious studies.[3]

Whatever else may be said about these developments, they have productively pushed the field toward greater engagement with the diverse range of human activities affiliated with "religion" as well as with the construction of the category itself. They have directed attention to the limits of conceiving religion principally in terms of either the doctrines articulated by theological elites or the ecstatic experiences so prominent in the work of figures as different as Rudolf Otto and William James. In their attention to knowledge and power, such studies have often been conducted with a genealogical cast,

---

[3] Asad, *Genealogies of Religion*, 29. Bruce Lincoln follows much of Asad's argument but rejects the conclusion that we must abandon the term religion; Bruce Lincoln, *Holy Terrors: Thinking about Religion after September 11*, 2nd edn. (Chicago: University of Chicago Press, 2006), 2. For comparable views, see Kevin Schilbrack, *Philosophy and the Study of Religions: A Manifesto* (Malden, MA: Wiley Blackwell, 2014), 85–111, and Jonathan Z. Smith, "Religion, Religions, Religious," in Taylor, *Critical Terms for Religious Studies*, 269–84. For an extraordinarily helpful account of many of these developments, which unpacks many of the distinctions to which I am only alluding here, see Constance M. Furey, "Body, Society, and Subjectivity in Religious Studies," *Journal of the American Academy of Religion* 80, no. 1 (2012): 7–33.

though one need not be a Foucaultian genealogist to appreciate the notion that "religion" is not a natural category and has developed historically, with great consequences.

Meanwhile, the term philosophy of religion has become deeply ambiguous. For many, the term designates a relatively discrete sub-field, which is itself subdivided into analytic and continental philosophy of religion, between which there is little traffic. In this narrower sense, philosophy of religion is fundamentally concerned with classic questions regarding the rationality of theism, such as theodicy, the nature of religious experience, and religious language.

While this notion of a distinct subfield continues to be well represented—perhaps dominant—in journal articles, edited volumes, and textbooks of classic readings, recent years have also seen the quiet emergence of a more diverse body of philosophically engaged scholarship on religion. Simultaneously, a number of important recent works in religious ethics have productively blurred the border between philosophy of religion and religious ethics. Despite the promise of these developments, however, they are just beginning to yield programmatic statements for a new vision of philosophy of religion.[4]

On the whole, then, despite noteworthy exceptions and some promising signs, philosophy of religion has not generated a substantial body of work that appreciates, engages with, and contributes to important broader developments in religious studies. For instance, I suspect that relatively little work in philosophy of religion from the last couple of decades finds its way onto recent theories and methods syllabi. Arguably no fundamentally philosophical work in the last quarter century has had the broad impact on religious studies of Wayne Proudfoot's *Religious Experience* (1985).[5] And work in philosophy of religion and

---

[4] Five recent works take important steps in this direction: Nancy K. Frankenberry, ed., *Radical Interpretation in Religion* (Cambridge: Cambridge University Press, 2002); Wesley Wildman, *Religious Philosophy as Multidisciplinary Comparative Inquiry: Envisioning a Future for the Philosophy of Religion* (Albany: State University of New York Press, 2010); G. Scott Davis, *Believing and Acting: The Pragmatic Turn in Comparative Religion and Ethics* (Oxford: Oxford University Press, 2012); Tyler T. Roberts, *Encountering Religion: Responsibility and Criticism after Secularism* (New York: Columbia University Press, 2013); and Kevin Schilbrack, *Philosophy and the Study of Religions*. The latter will be an important conversation partner, both implicitly and explicitly, throughout this project.

[5] Wayne Proudfoot, *Religious Experience* (Berkeley: University of California Press, 1985).

ethics is rarely classed among the exciting research that has implications for religious studies as a whole.

The results, I contend, have been bad for everyone. Philosophy of religion has generally failed to engage with productive developments in the broader field of religious studies—such as attention to the historical construction of the category of religion—while these developments themselves have suffered from too little engagement with philosophers of religion and scholars of religious thought. Philosophically oriented analyses of the Western construction of religion, for instance, will reveal much more nuance and diversity within even the more canonical works than critics often contend. And such treatments, far from being mere footnotes to our understanding of classics, shed crucial light on the social worlds we inhabit today. The accounts of religion's modern formations and how we study them—to which scholars such as Robert Orsi, Saba Mahmood, Thomas Tweed, and Manuel Vásquez have contributed so much—cannot do without this kind of philosophical work on religion.[6]

A VISION IN BRIEF

This book seeks to address this gap between philosophy of religion and the broader field of religious studies. Many philosophers of religion find ourselves entirely at home in neither analytic nor continental philosophy of religion. Although we may share much of analytic philosophy's aspiration to clarity, our work does not engage centrally with the vocabulary or the body of literature that has come to define analytic philosophy of religion. And while a number of us deal extensively with thinkers from the European continent, we do not locate our work in the specific trajectory of post-Heideggerian thought that has come to function as the canon of continental philosophy of religion.

---

[6] Robert A. Orsi, *Between Heaven and Earth: The Religious Worlds People Make and the Scholars Who Study Them* (Princeton: Princeton University Press, 2005); Saba Mahmood, *Politics of Piety: The Islamic Revival and the Feminist Subject* (Princeton: Princeton University Press, 2005); Thomas A. Tweed, *Crossing and Dwelling: A Theory of Religion* (Cambridge: Harvard University Press, 2006); and Vásquez, *More than Belief.*

Taking this newly emerging scholarship seriously expands the category of philosophy of religion in terms of the traditions considered, the genres of writing examined, the significance of attention to historical figures, and the probing of the concept of religion itself. The result moves beyond a conception of philosophy of religion as dominated by philosophical analysis of classic questions regarding the rationality of theism. In offering a programmatic vision of philosophy of religion that awards such work a central role, I contend that *philosophy of religion should be conceived less in terms of a fixed set of questions than in terms of philosophical modes of analysis of a range of questions and topics generated both by the study of particular religions and by the process of studying religion itself.* Philosophy of religion so understood is not only attentive to a range of questions generated by diverse religious traditions but also self-conscious about the category of religion itself—including its history—and the way that this and other categories frame our questions and studies in the first place.

In probing what philosophy of religion should be learning from as well as contributing to religious studies as a whole, I hope to speak not only to philosophers of religion but to a broader audience of students and scholars interested in philosophy's role in the study of religion. Although the book is centrally concerned with articulating a conception of philosophy of religion adequate to religious studies, i.e., the academic study of religion, it also addresses what philosophy of religion as a whole—including as practiced in departments of philosophy—should learn from recent developments in religious studies. Toward this end, I do not want to separate work in philosophy of religion done by scholars in departments of philosophy, religious studies, or other institutional homes.[7] The issues I take up in this book should be of concern to philosophers of

---

[7] Empirically speaking, philosophy of religion done by scholars in departments of philosophy is often quite different from that done by scholars in departments of religious studies and/or theology. This division also frequently corresponds to the distinction between analytic and continental philosophy of religion. Although these patterns are not random, they are not intellectually justified. Moreover, even as empirical tendencies, they have their limits: the Philosophy of Religion Section of the American Academy of Religion, in its leadership as well as panels, spans these divisions; and a great deal of important work in philosophy of religion is done by people whose institutional homes do not fit these patterns. More importantly, it is always dangerous to allow departmental distinctions to function as defensive barriers that excuse us from confronting legitimate challenges to our assumptions.

religion regardless of their institutional setting, as well as to scholars of religion more broadly.

Moreover, the contributions that philosophy of religion can and should make to topics such as the history of the conceptualization of religion, the concept and nature of tradition, and the nature of comparative inquiry, are no less significant for extra-disciplinary audiences. Within the academy, religion has newly or renewedly become a major topic of inquiry in political science, economics, anthropology, cognitive science, literature, and history, to name a few areas. Beyond the academy, the methodological and theoretical debates about religion that have recently been so prominent in religious studies scholarship are no less important to broader public discourse about religion. These are not a matter of "merely academic" precision or details. As I highlight in Chapter 5, they pertain directly to how we comprehend and confront the most urgent of our global conflicts. Thus, as much as this project takes off from the recent history of academic subfields, it seeks to be relevant to a broader range of students, scholars, and other interested parties.

SOME PRELIMINARY CONCEPTIONS

In speaking of the "academic study of religion" or "religious studies," I mean to distinguish this form of the study of religion from certain other kinds—such as work in which particular religious commitments are taken for granted. I understand the academic study of religion as the disciplined examination of religion, including religious thought, people, movements, practices, materials, etc., as well as reflection on the conceptions of each of these terms, without presupposing the validity of or privileging the study of any particular religion or group of religious phenomena. Conceived in this manner, religious studies does not presuppose the truth of any particular claims—or of some purported "religion in general." Crucially, neither does it presuppose their falsity. As I argue at length in Chapter 2, the field should not be thought of in terms of religious studies over against theology. Work in theology is too diverse to be designated as always belonging to or always excluded from religious studies: some legitimately belongs (and fits within the expansive vision of philosophy of religion that I offer); some excludes itself by making conversation-stopping appeals to authorities conceived as unquestionable. Nor should we conceive work in religious studies as "non-normative," over against work that belongs only in seminaries. To the contrary, normativity is pervasive, in history and philosophy as well as religious studies; normativity should not be avoided but rather self-consciously acknowledged and defended. Instead, what is crucial to the study of religion's being academic is a principled willingness to submit all claims to scrutiny and questioning, to insist that no assumptions, doctrines, or authorities are beyond questioning.

Concretely, various religions are studied and none is endowed with a privileged status. While individual studies will focus on specific instances of religion, perhaps particular religions, the same cannot be said for religious studies as a whole. Moreover, the kinds of evidence to which one appeals are not different from those appealed to in other areas of the humanities or social sciences—even though, as is the case in many disciplines, there may be robust debate about what counts as evidence. The methods or approaches employed will be diverse, with some scholars of religion closely connected to other fields such as history, anthropology, sociology, literary studies, philosophy, and so forth. Finally, religious studies possesses an evolving, loosely defined body of literature reflecting on the study of religion, as suggested in the opening pages of this Introduction. Of course, like any discipline, religious studies can also be analyzed in terms of its institutional presences: journals, books series, professional organizations, and conferences as well as departments and programs of religion or religious studies. In the present context, however, there are important reasons to focus instead on the considerations already mentioned.

To be sure, no individual study will do all of these things. It is vital to distinguish the boundaries and expectations relevant to the discipline as a whole from those that are appropriate for an individual work of scholarship. The former circumscribe a large sphere of inquiry, the latter a small subset of the former. Though the field of religious studies should not systematically privilege Christianity, for instance, it is not inappropriate for individual studies to focus on a particular Christian movement and, in this very limited sense, to privilege the study of Christianity. But Christianity is no different from Buddhism or Islam in this respect. Moreover, the question of whether particular works belong in the field of religious studies is very different from the question of whether I agree with the claims made or see a general approach as promising. There is a good deal of work on religion that I suspect to be headed toward a dead end but that I would not want to rule out of the bounds of the discipline.

In developing a vision of "philosophy of religion," this book focuses on the construction of the second term more than the first. Nonetheless, some discussion of "philosophy" is in order. Conceptions of philosophy might be organized in terms of attention to one or more of three elements: (1) the modes of analysis, (2) the objects or topics of analysis, and (3) a specific history or histories of inquiry. In the present context, I take the first of these to be the most important. I have in mind modes of analysis that critically probe the nature of argument and the details of the arguments themselves. Philosophical analysis interrogates the presuppositions and assesses the validity of particular arguments as well as examines what it means to give good reasons. Regarding the second element, the objects or topics of analysis, a central thrust of this book is that the traditional topics of philosophy of religion have been too narrow. Accordingly, the emerging vision of philosophy of religion will both expand beyond topics such as epistemology and metaphysics and be defined less in terms of its topics than its modes of analysis. Third, the history of the discourse of philosophy of religion, particularly in recent decades, has been similarly narrow; I argue that we need to expand the canon. Nonetheless, part of the point of labeling this field philosophy of religion is to highlight the connections to histories of inquiry under that rubric, particularly if we stretch back to the early modern period. While some are tempted to abandon "philosophy of religion" in favor of "critical theory of religion," holding on to the term philosophy of religion productively illuminates the continuity between this work and the history of philosophical inquiry as well as challenges the unjustified boundaries that do much to fragment discussions that belong together.

THE ROAD AHEAD

In order to probe philosophy of religion's role in religious studies, the book consists in a series of interventions, each intended to prod the development of the field in a particular aspect—always working against the gap that exists between much work in philosophy of religion and important recent developments that speak to religious studies as a whole. Providing a context and justification for these individual studies requires a consideration of the broader landscape of philosophy of religion today. With that goal in mind, Chapter 1 examines the contemporary state of philosophy of religion. I consider the prominent division of the field into analytic and continental philosophy of religion, noting the strengths as well as the narrowness of much of the work that falls under these rubrics. Having noted these literatures' neglect of critical questions around the concept of religion, I then turn to three recent works that illustrate more promising directions for philosophy of religion: Amy Hollywood's *Sensible Ecstasy: Mysticism, Sexual Difference, and the Demands of History*; Jonathon Kahn's *Divine Discontent: The Religious Imagination of W. E. B. Du Bois*; and Dan Arnold's *Brains, Buddhas, and Believing: The Problem of Intentionality in Classical Buddhist and Cognitive-Scientific Philosophy of Mind.*[8] Despite the tremendous differences among them, none of these books fit easily into the conversations of either analytic or continental philosophy of religion. Each, in different ways, productively probes the boundaries of the concept of religion in ways that contribute to broader discussions in religious studies and demonstrates the promise of work in philosophy of religion that moves in these directions.

Chapter 2 takes up the question of normativity. In recent years, one of the significant obstacles to philosophy of religion's integration in the field of religious studies has been widespread suspicion of its making normative claims. This objection to normativity has often been set out in terms of a contrast between "theology" (which is understood as normative) and "religious studies" (which is not). Against such claims, I argue that neither of these framings is adequate to determine what work does and does not belong in the academic study of religion. To the contrary, normativity is pervasive—in the work of historians and anthropologists as well as philosophers of religion. What distinguishes philosophy of religion and religious ethics from these other subfields is not that they are uniquely

---

[8] Amy M. Hollywood, *Sensible Ecstasy: Mysticism, Sexual Difference, and the Demands of History* (Chicago: University of Chicago Press, 2002); Jonathon S. Kahn, *Divine Discontent: The Religious Imagination of W. E. B. Du Bois* (Oxford: Oxford University Press, 2009); and Dan Arnold, *Brains, Buddhas, and Believing: The Problem of Intentionality in Classical Buddhist and Cognitive-Scientific Philosophy of Mind* (New York: Columbia University Press, 2012).

normative but that they are often explicit in their reflection on their normative claims. With regard to inclusion in the academic study of religion, what matters is not whether a scholar is normative but whether she or he is in principle willing to offer arguments in support of those normative claims rather than to engage in conversation-stopping appeals to fixed authorities.

The next chapter brings together two recent turns to history: attention within philosophy of religion to major figures in its past, on one hand, and a turn to the history of the conceptualization of religion within broader methodological discussions in religious studies, on the other. In doing so, this chapter examines what philosophy of religion might learn from recent work on the history of the study of religion. Through a comparative treatment of Friedrich Schleiermacher and G. W. F. Hegel, I argue that conceiving of the contributions of influential figures in the modern history of the philosophy of religion as attempting to transform the contested category of religion itself both highlights the importance of historical study to philosophy of religion and illuminates the centrality of philosophy of religion to religious studies as a whole.

Chapter 4 turns toward religious ethics. Given the beneficial blurring of boundaries between philosophy of religion and religious ethics in recent years, we can expect that many of the most productive directions for these subfields will be ones that do not separate them. With this point in mind, an examination of the future of the philosophy of religion should also attend to religious ethics. Both participants and observers often conceive of "comparative religious ethics" (CRE) as a distinct subfield within the larger field of religious ethics. Against this conception, I argue that it is time to move beyond thinking of a separate subfield for studies of two or more figures, texts, or groups. Instead, religious ethics as a whole should appreciate the methodological fruits of the body of literature labeled CRE over the last several decades—in particular the realization of the extent to which all interpretation involves comparison as well as the import of the work done in the scholar's own mind. The resulting vision of religious ethics further undermines the hegemony of Christianity within religious ethics by engaging a variety of traditions and bringing that engagement into a common conversation whose guiding concepts and categories are continually supplemented and expanded through encounters with materials from a wide range of contexts.

The final chapter turns outward, considering the public impact of the study of religion. September 11 marks—among many other things—a watershed in the place of religion in the university. Previously, many judged religion to be a relic of merely historical or personal interest. Early in the last decade, however, many scholars across the university came to see religion as worthy of study. One influential response has been a call for "religious literacy." In *Religious Literacy: What Every American Needs to Know—And Doesn't*, Stephen Prothero argues for the importance of learning "basic facts" about various religions.[9] Against this influential vision, I argue that religious literacy so conceived is not just inadequate; it is profoundly misleading and sets back our quest to understand religion's contemporary significance. If we imagine that such knowledge constitutes the beginning of religious literacy (or "the basics"), we implicitly take for granted that religion is first and foremost a matter of subscribing to a set of claims contained in a body of texts that are taken to be uniquely authoritative. That understanding of religion leaves us dramatically unprepared to comprehend the myriad, complex ways that religion functions in people's lives. Identifying these shortcomings in Prothero's project simultaneously directs our attention to the way that the broader field of religious studies remains constrained by notions of discrete religious traditions that do more organizational work than they should. Driving currents in in the field should push us further and further from such views of religions. Among other factors, attention to particular groups and individuals has not simply deepened the appreciation of differences within a single so-called tradition but also called into question religious "traditions" as meaningful units of analysis. While we need not abandon rubrics such as "Christian," "Muslim," "Hindu," and "Buddhist," we should be much more self-conscious about the roles they play in structuring the study of religion.

The conclusion weaves together the contributions developed over the previous chapters to articulate the resulting vision of philosophy of religion and its significance for the broader field of religious studies. I focus particularly on the conjunction of history and normativity that forms a persistent thread through the book. Hegel and Nietzsche can be seen as paradigmatic for the two dominant options

---

[9] Stephen Prothero, *Religious Literacy: What Every American Needs to Know—And Doesn't* (San Francisco: HarperOne, 2008).

for theorizing the significance of history for normative work. Drawing on non-traditional readings of Hegel enables us to avoid the grandest charges against him, even if it by no means eliminates all concerns about judging others. Ultimately, I contend, Hegel provides greater resources than Nietzsche for engaging our histories—including their triumphs and exclusions—in relation to our present commitments, ongoing arguments, and future prospects.

1

Landscapes, Lacunae, and Prospects

Mapping the landscape of recent work in philosophy of religion is necessarily tentative but nonetheless necessary. It is tentative because mapping a field inevitably requires preliminary judgments about what material ought to be included in the map. It already invokes assumptions about which work does and does not belong. At worst, it might appear that the inquiry's outcome has been decided before the investigation begins. Yet we can only fully appreciate the significance of new directions if we have a sense of the current shape of the field; only such a picture can identify the lacunae that merit attention. Surveying the landscape thus provides an invaluable context for making interventions.

This chapter seeks to identify major tendencies, features, and directions in the bodies of literature most readily and widely identified under the rubric of philosophy of religion. Since the guiding purpose is to identify gaps and thin points in the discussion, we need not be overly concerned about a precise delineation of borders. In surveying the state of "philosophy of religion," I rely less on my own views of what philosophy of religion should be than on how people identify their work. My hope is that this strategy largely dissipates worries that this initial portrayal of the landscape might over-determine the conclusions drawn.[1] Although I do not aspire to comprehensiveness,

---

[1] In the present context, I believe dissipation is the most we should aim for. The treatment that follows does leave out important work that I ultimately consider part of philosophy of religion. To mention only one example, much recent scholarship in modern Jewish thought seems to me to belong in the category and frequently shares important features with promising work I consider at the end of this chapter. Not to attend more closely to this body of literature may therefore make the situation of philosophy of religion appear more dire than it is. Moreover, questions raised by the nomenclature of "modern Jewish thought" rather than "modern Jewish philosophy"

I bring together work done by scholars in divinity schools as well as departments of philosophy, religious studies, and (occasionally) related fields. While the conversations undertaken by scholars in departments of philosophy and those in departments of religious studies frequently appear to be radically separate, I see no satisfactory rationale for this separation; more importantly, I worry when such institutional factors provide excuses for neglecting questions that ought to be asked. For this reason, I believe it is important to present these discussions as parts of a potentially integrated field in which all participants are held responsible for addressing concerns raised by other participants—not excused because that potential interlocutor is housed in a different department.[2]

I organize this overview largely in terms of two camps—analytic and continental—and argue that, despite their vast differences, they are united in their relative neglect of broader developments in religious studies. Building on this identification of lacunae, I then turn to three works that suggest promising prospects for the field: Amy Hollywood's *Sensible Ecstasy: Mysticism, Sexual Difference, and the Demands of History*; Jonathon Kahn's *Divine Discontent: The Religious Imagination of W. E. B. Du Bois*; and Dan Arnold's *Brains, Buddhas, and Believing: The Problem of Intentionality in Classical Buddhist and Cognitive-Scientific Philosophy of Mind*.[3] I treat these works from an atypical angle, seeking to sketch the kinds of contributions they make—not to provide overall accounts of them. I thus

certainly relate closely to the issues of this chapter. For instance, has philosophy of religion been constructed in a manner that excludes many of the methods and topics prominent in "modern Jewish thought"? While the obvious answer is yes, the more pressing question concerns how deep these exclusions run. My view is that the developments in the field recommended in this book do not simply provide an opening for modern Jewish thought to be considered part of philosophy of religion but rather implicitly suggest that much work under this rubric may be seen as paradigmatic for having overcome many of the limits of much work in philosophy of religion. Nonetheless, these considerations do not undermine my principal claims regarding the shape of what is widely identified as "philosophy of religion" today. I am grateful to Sarah Hammerschlag for making me think further on these issues.

[2] On this issue, see the Introduction, note 7.

[3] Amy M. Hollywood, *Sensible Ecstasy: Mysticism, Sexual Difference, and the Demands of History* (Chicago: University of Chicago Press, 2002); Jonathon S. Kahn, *Divine Discontent: The Religious Imagination of W. E. B. Du Bois* (Oxford: Oxford University Press, 2009); and Dan Arnold, *Brains, Buddhas, and Believing: The Problem of Intentionality in Classical Buddhist and Cognitive-Scientific Philosophy of Mind* (New York: Columbia University Press, 2012).

focus on the features of these books that address the lacunae revealed by our survey and that represent fruitful directions for philosophy of religion.

ANALYTIC PHILOSOPHY OF RELIGION AND RELIGIOUS STUDIES

Examining the bulk of contemporary scholarship that identifies itself under the rubric of philosophy of religion reveals a curious situation: a field that appears simultaneously deeply divided and strikingly homogeneous. On one side of this division lies analytic philosophy of religion. In many respects, analytic philosophy of religion has experienced a remarkable renaissance in recent decades, if largely in departments of philosophy rather than of religious studies. After a near-death experience at the hands of logical positivism in the first half of the twentieth century, Anglo-American analytic philosophy of religion began a slow but steady recovery in the mid-1950s. *New Essays in Philosophical Theology*, edited by Antony Flew and Alasdair MacIntyre in 1955, marks the beginning of this resurgence, which gradually gained momentum and remains vital today.[4] Whereas logical positivism's dominance in English-speaking philosophy had convinced many philosophers that religious language was meaning-less, subsequent developments in analytic philosophy have challenged that presumption from a number of different directions. The result-ing proliferation has driven diverse developments in this subfield, such that circumscribing "analytic philosophy of religion" in terms of commonly held commitments (whether methodological or substan-tive) has become challenging. Nicholas Wolterstorff has influentially argued that the field is best grasped in terms of a narrative, and Michael Rae's account makes the engagement with a particular body of literature (not shared substantive commitments) integral to

---

[4] While a number of works offer brief sketches of the twentieth-century history of analytic philosophy of religion, I have found particularly helpful William Hasker, "Analytic Philosophy of Religion," in *The Oxford Handbook of Philosophy of Religion*, ed. William J. Wainwright, Oxford Handbooks in Philosophy (Oxford: Oxford University Press, 2005), 421–46. See also Nicholas Wolterstorff, *Inquiring about God: Selected Essays, Vol. 1*, ed. Terence Cuneo (Cambridge: Cambridge University Press, 2010), 17–34.

his conception of analytic philosophy of religion.[5] In this respect, methodological and substantive views arguably do less to distinguish analytic philosophy of religion than the engagement with a particular tradition of inquiry.

Within this body of literature constituting analytic philosophy of religion, several features stand out. Reflecting tendencies in modern philosophy as a whole and analytic philosophy in particular, questions about the rationality of religious belief, and thus epistemology, have consistently been a major concern. Analytic philosophy of religion is often accused of a form of ahistoricism that accepts the criterion that a satisfactory argument must appeal to human beings universally. This accusation, however, fails to do justice to central developments in the field. As Wolterstorff highlights, most analytic philosophers of religion today have abandoned the aspiration to "confine themselves to premises that all normal, adult, appropriately informed human beings would accept if those premises were presented to them and they understood them."[6] While this development tracks broader developments in philosophy, the movement known as Reformed Epistemology, which holds that religious beliefs can themselves be basic (rather than in need of support from more fundamental sources of evidence), has done much to promote this shift within analytic philosophy of religion. (This is not to say, however, that all analytic philosophers of religion have abandoned attempts to convince the skeptical: Richard Swinburne, for instance, famously builds a partly mathematical argument for the probability of Jesus's resurrection.[7]) For many, however, this epistemological development has enabled them to set aside classic modern demands that religious beliefs must be grounded in something more epistemically fundamental than these beliefs themselves.

In doing so, Reformed Epistemology has helped clear the way for a return to engagement with classic metaphysical claims about the

---

[5] Wolterstorff, *Inquiring about God*, 17, and Michael C. Rea, "Introduction," in *Analytic Theology: New Essays in the Philosophy of Theology*, ed. Oliver D. Crisp and Michael C. Rea (Oxford: Oxford University Press, 2009), 3–6.

[6] Wolterstorff, *Inquiry about God*, 7. See also Nicholas Wolterstorff, "Reformed Epistemology," in *Practices of Belief: Selected Essays, Vol. 2*, ed. Terence Cuneo (Cambridge: Cambridge University Press, 2010), 334–49.

[7] Richard Swinburne, "The Probability of the Resurrection," in *God and the Ethics of Belief: New Essays in Philosophy of Religion*, ed. Andrew Dole and Andrew Chignell (Cambridge: Cambridge University Press, 2005), 117–30.

existence and nature of God. Whereas moving beyond logical positivism increased confidence that religious language need not be meaningless, Reformed Epistemology has supported the idea that arguments about such topics are not doomed to failure. Rejecting Kantian accounts of the limits of theoretical reason, recent work in analytic philosophy of religion has engaged extensively with proofs for the existence of God and other classic questions about theism.[8] And while some of these points are not necessarily distinctly Christian (a point to which I return below), recent work has also come to engage more and more with specific Christian doctrinal claims, such as notions of the Trinity or Christology.[9]

Clearing away Kantian obstacles to knowledge of God has also supported analytic philosophers in returning to pre-modern, particularly medieval, theological projects. Where an earlier generation might have held that Kant rendered much of this material obsolete for the philosophically inclined, not so today. For this and other reasons, analytic philosophy of religion has begun to engage more with the history of philosophy and theology. At present, however, this development is still new, and it remains to be seen how far these historically oriented tendencies will develop: at present analytic philosophy of religion remains predominantly occupied with a post-1950s body of literature.

Although Reformed Epistemology may have helped clear the way for a return to pre-Kantian materials—and thus contributed to greater engagement with history—other aspects of this development may function as a brake on more extensive engagement with historical sources. Perhaps most significantly, in eschewing aspirations to appeal to all rational interlocutors, much recent work in analytic philosophy of religion has focused on the more precise articulation and unpacking of commitments already held. Linking these points together, Wolterstorff has written:

---

[8] At the same time, a number of scholars have challenged the dominant readings of Kant and argued for a "more metaphysical" Kant. See Chris L. Firestone and Stephen R. Palmquist, eds., *Kant and the New Philosophy of Religion* (Bloomington: Indiana University Press, 2006); Chris L. Firestone and Nathan Jacobs, *In Defense of Kant's Religion* (Bloomington: Indiana University Press, 2008); and John Hare, *The Moral Gap* (Oxford: Clarendon Press, 1996).

[9] See, for instance, Oliver D. Crisp and Michael C. Rea, eds., *Analytic Theology: New Essays in the Philosophy of Theology* (Oxford: Oxford University Press, 2009); Wolterstorff, *Inquiring about God*.

The majority of recent analytic philosophers of religion have not supposed that one could or should practice philosophy as a generic human being, appealing solely to reason. They have regarded philosophy in general, not just philosophy of religion, as in good measure and in various ways an articulation of one's own particular perspective. That is why these philosophers have neither tried to shed nor to conceal the religious convictions that they bring to philosophy.... They have not only been willing to *describe* religion from within; they have *practiced philosophy of religion* from within.[10]

Critiques of the universalist aspirations of classical foundationalism thus underwrite a conception of the practice of philosophy more as the unpacking of the baggage one already carries than the questioning of whether one should hold on to these bags. Of course, it would be a mistake to overemphasize the contrast: the two options are not mutually exclusive. To focus on the first task does not render the second concern illegitimate. Nonetheless, for much analytic philosophy of religion, the former task can be pursued at the expense of the latter. More specifically, such work frequently not only rejects the possibility of a universalistic standpoint for critique but also forgoes other ways of interrogating the presuppositions involved in the religious claims that are taken to be epistemically basic.[11]

One result can be that this focus on unpacking the scholar's own standpoint makes the study of history propaedeutic to that task in a way at odds with the deep engagement in historical materials—thickly situated in their own contexts—that allows them to *challenge* our views, not simply to unpack them. Another frequent though not necessary consequence is a narrow focus on Christian topics and concerns. At a minimum, we can say that the result is an insufficiently inclusive vision of what philosophy of religion could and should be in religious studies. More is needed.

Whereas a good deal of analytic philosophy of religion is explicit about its distinctly Christian focus, some work in this tradition intends to speak about religion more generally. Even here, however, the Christian background of the conversation is often apparent.

[10] Wolterstorff, *Inquiring about God*, 19.

[11] In other words, the Hegelian vision I sketch in the Conclusion offers important additional resources for questioning whether we ought to consider discarding some of our baggage—without relying on appeals to the kinds of foundationalism that are here being critiqued.

Broad treatments of the rationality of theism often illustrate this point well. While the question obviously has deep roots in Christian conversations, contemporary philosophers of religion are quick to point out its broader relevance. Even if the authors on whom they draw have been shaped largely by Christianity, they justify the importance of their work by noting the significance of theism in other traditions as well. They frequently acknowledge other religions only in noting that they too deal with these same issues. To take one illustrative example, the majority of Charles Taliaferro's entry on "Philosophy of Religion" in the *Stanford Encyclopedia of Philosophy* deals with questions about the notion and rationality of theism. In the opening paragraph of the section, he contends that:

> The emergence and development of Judaism, Christianity and Islam on a global scale secured the centrality of theism for philosophical enquiry, but the relevance of a philosophical exploration of theism is not limited to those interested in these religions and the cultures in which they flourish. While theism has generally flourished in religious traditions amid religious practices, one may be a theist without adopting any religion whatever, and one may find theistic elements (however piecemeal) in Confucianism, Hinduism, some versions of Mahayana Buddhism, as well as in the religions of some smaller scale societies. The debate over theism also has currency for secular humanism and religious forms of atheism as in Theravada Buddhist philosophy.[12]

While I find no need to quarrel with Taliaferro's claims, what is significant about his and others' *uses* of this kind of claim is that they function to justify the significance of the project without actually informing the project. That is, after making this point, they proceed to discuss arguments about theism in virtually the same way they might have had they only been talking about Christian accounts of God. Some exceptions occur insofar as authors make occasional references to arguments by Jewish or Muslim thinkers, but these exceptions only highlight the larger pattern. Substantively, they proceed in a way that makes it unclear whether the inclusion of these

---

[12] Charles Taliaferro, "Philosophy of Religion," *The Stanford Encyclopedia of Philosophy* (Spring 2011 Edition), Edward N. Zalta (ed.), URL = <http://plato.stanford.edu/archives/spr2011/entries/philosophy-religion/>. For other examples, see Linda Trinkaus Zagzebski, *Philosophy of Religion: An Historical Introduction* (Malden, MA: Blackwell Publishing, 2007), section 1.2.1, and William Mann, ed., *The Blackwell Guide to the Philosophy of Religion* (Malden, MA: Blackwell, 2005), x and xiv.

traditions makes any difference. With regard to substance, the efforts to move the academic study of religion beyond the presumption that Christianity is the principal object of study have largely passed this strand of philosophy of religion by.

These limited bounds of much writing in analytic philosophy of religion reflect the powerful work done by the largely implicit notions of religion that circumscribe the questions and the data set. In other words, the topics and the body of literature through which these topics are elaborated and investigated are largely an inheritance from Christian theology. The underlying understanding of what religion *is* is frequently taken over implicitly and uncritically from the history of Christian thought.

Responding to some analytic philosophers' own recognition of the paucity of attention to the concept of religion, one recent effort to broaden the frame of analytic philosophy of religion—with particular attention to the concept of religion—deserves special mention. J. L. Schellenberg's *Prolegomena to a Philosophy of Religion* intends to fill this lacuna. Precisely here, however, the costs of so little engagement with the broader discipline of religious studies become apparent. Schellenberg begins his project by examining the importance of defining the concept of religion. It is sometimes unclear whether he aspires to a definition capturing an essence of religion or one that simply enables us to communicate clearly; at a key point, however, he advocates a "technical" definition that he views as uniquely appropriate to philosophy of religion, above all because it focuses on matters (those surrounding what he calls ultimacy) that he deems to be "*clearly* at the heart of *philosophy*."[13] The claim raises a number of issues: To conceive the definition of religion in terms of the term philosophy, for instance, seems to inordinately constrain the notion of a philosophical examination of religion. Instead, I would argue that the object of philosophical analysis (here, "religion") should be determined relatively independently of the mode of analysis itself (i.e., philosophy). Philosophical work can and should determine how we conceptualize religion—that is part of my point—but it should not do so simply by stipulating the definition of religion to accord with pre-established notions of the topics or object of philosophy.

---

[13] J. L. Schellenberg, *Prolegomena to a Philosophy of Religion* (Ithaca: Cornell University Press, 2005), 24, emphasis in original.

More significantly, his efforts to develop a definition display a remarkable lack of familiarity with the scholarship on this topic. He claims in the footnote on the first page of the preface that "relatively little reflection has been devoted to determining exactly what faith is and what makes a state of belief religious."[14] For anyone vaguely familiar with the reams of writing on these topics in religious studies, the statement is striking. When he turns toward articulating his own definition, he takes his orientation from William James and Wilfred Cantwell Smith, using them to justify what he takes to be a basic distinction between "*personal* and *institutional* or, if you like, *internal* and *external*" senses of religion.[15] Within another two pages, he has dismissed "institutional" aspects of religion as secondary to "personal" aspects and therewith dismissed "institutional" religion as outside the focus of the inquiry. While there is still much to be said for the work of James and W. C. Smith, their views have been widely criticized in the half century since the latter wrote. More significantly, precisely the effort to separate "personal" and "institutional" senses of religion exemplifies the kind of move that numerous scholars in recent decades have associated with the covert insertion of specific Protestant presuppositions into purportedly universal definitions of religion.[16] One of the major concerns raised in recent religious studies scholarship (e.g., J. Z. Smith, Talal Asad, Tomoko Masuzawa, Daniel Dubuisson) is that the inordinate focus on faith and/or belief— exemplified in Schellenberg's work—leads to the neglect of practical and material aspects of religion. No less importantly, by trying to fix the concept of religion in the opening pages of a prolegomena to philosophy of religion (dismissing everything but "personal" or "internal" religion by page six of a three-volume work), Schellenberg largely removes the history of the conceptualization of religion from the field of vision of work in philosophy of religion.

The result is a vision of philosophy of religion that—despite Schellenberg's explicit aspirations to broaden the scope—has learned little from and has little to contribute to broader developments in the study

---

[14] Schellenberg, *Prolegomena*, ix n. 1.

[15] Schellenberg, *Prolegomena*, 4, emphasis in original.

[16] The same point can be made about Linda Zagzebski's appeal to the work of Rudolf Otto as she sets out the definition of religion that will operate in her work; Zagzebski, *Philosophy of Religion*, 4.

of religion.[17] While Schellenberg might hope to neutralize some of these criticisms by virtue of his focus on a technical definition gauged to fit with the concerns he takes to be central to philosophy itself, this is a rather narrow vision of philosophy. (Think, for instance, of the way that it marginalizes attention to ethical formation.) Insofar as Schellenberg responds that these are the particular aspects of philosophy that interest him (and, to be fair, many others), he has ceded the claim to provide a prolegomena to philosophy of religion in general. It may be appropriate to stipulate such a narrow definition for the sake of the inquiry that a particular scholar seeks to pursue, but that is no reason to define the subfield in this manner. As long as it is conceived in this way, philosophy of religion will remain a parochial endeavor.

In making these points about much recent work in analytic philosophy of religion, I in no sense want to argue against the legitimacy or importance of work in this area. Moreover, by circumscribing the topics so narrowly, work in this field can be seen as gaining important traction and developing a community of inquiry. Nonetheless, my point in highlighting these limits is to argue that work along these lines should not be taken to comprise the entirety of "philosophy of religion" within the academic study of religion. Insofar as it does, other scholars of religion can justifiably contend that it is dominated by Christian apologetic concerns and their criticism; vis-à-vis religious studies as a whole, which seeks not to privilege any particular religion, it appears parochial. Moreover, it remains an autonomous subfield that neither contributes to nor benefits from the broader study of religion. Thus, to limit philosophy of religion to these topics and methods dramatically limits the significance of philosophy for the academic study of religion. Philosophy's role in religious studies can and should be greater.

---

[17] Regarding Schellenberg's attempts to expand the conception of philosophy of religion, see his discussion of "ultimization" (e.g., 25) and his proposal for expanding the aims of philosophy of religion (184–94). Yet the account of ultimization cannot but recall Paul Tillich's extensively critiqued account of religion in terms of ultimate concern. And the somewhat expanded aims of philosophy of religion still make it the subfield's priority to consider "the challenge that *nonreligious responses to religious claims are rationally preferable to religious ones*" (Schellenberg, *Prolegomena*, 193, emphasis in original). As significant as this question is, it is hardly a radical departure from a great deal of other work in analytic philosophy of religion.

CONTINENTAL PHILOSOPHY OF RELIGION
AND RELIGIOUS STUDIES

In light of these limits to analytic philosophy of religion, it is note-worthy that work in continental philosophy of religion frequently presents itself precisely as expanding beyond the boundaries of ana-lytic philosophy of religion. In a chapter entitled "Continental Phil-osophy of Religion: An Introduction," for instance, Philip Goodchild begins by defining continental philosophy of religion in contrast to "philosophy of religion in English-speaking countries, [which]... focuses largely on the truth-claims, rationality, and coherence of religious propositions, and particularly those of 'classical theism.'"[18] Continental philosophy of religion is introduced as engaging questions beyond these narrow bounds and challenging the conceptions of reason taken as fundamental to analytic philosophy of religion. Con-tinental philosophy of religion is thus presented as the other that exposes and transgresses the limits of analytic philosophy of religion.[19]

In doing so, "continental philosophy of religion" draws upon a particular line of twentieth- and twenty-first-century German and French thought that opposes the models of reason dominant in analytic philosophy. The resulting new canon makes references to figures such as Kant, Hegel, and Nietzsche but begins in earnest with Martin Heidegger and draws heavily on his appropriation by French thinkers such as Emmanuel Levinas and Jacques Derrida. "Contin-ental" is thus used in a very specific sense here, referring to a line of thought developing out of Heidegger.[20] In this sense, for much recent work that identifies itself as "continental philosophy of religion," Kant and Hegel hardly count as "continental" thinkers.[21] Although

---

[18] Philip Goodchild, "Continental Philosophy of Religion: An Introduction," in *Rethinking Philosophy of Religion: Approaches from Continental Philosophy*, ed. Philip Goodchild (New York: Fordham University Press, 2002), 1.

[19] Nick Trakakis's *The End of Philosophy of Religion* (London: Continuum, 2008) presents another instance of this conception of continental philosophy of religion as valuably exceeding the limits of an overly narrow analytic philosophy of religion.

[20] For instance, while Goodchild initially notes that " '[c]ontinental philosophy' is a phrase commonly used in the English-speaking world to describe a tradition of thought deriving from Kant, Hegel, Marx, Nietzsche, and Freud...," when he actually gets down to discussing the key figures for this continental philosophy of religion, he begins with Heidegger. See Goodchild, "Continental Philosophy of Religion," 14–16.

[21] To be sure, Kant sometimes figures as particularly important for having recog-nized a need to limit the claims of theoretical reason to make room for faith.

I find this nomenclature questionable, I will use "continental philosophy of religion" to refer specifically to scholarship coming out of
this Heideggerian and post-Heideggerian line rather than for all work
that engages centrally with thinkers from the European continent.
Viewed from this perspective, even though continental philosophy
can be seen as centrally engaged with the history of the philosophy of
religion, it is—for the most part—a very specific history.

More significantly, the specificity of this history generates another
crucial feature of much work in continental philosophy of religion.
Engagement with religion is here largely motivated by—or at least
developed in tandem with—a view about the limits of reason. Roughly
put, in the face of reason's failure, we turn to religion. Religion is thus
conceived as reason's other. While construing reason in such terms is
by no means unique to continental philosophy of religion, neither is it
universal. To take it as foundational for the conception of philosophy
of religion is to allow a particular, post-Enlightenment, Western trajectory of thinking about religion to circumscribe the field. This narrow
historical scope undergirds an overly narrow conceptual scope—one
inadequate to conceiving of philosophy of religion in a manner
adequate to the breadth of the academic study of religion today. As
with analytic philosophy of religion, good work may be done within
this frame, but the frame is too small to appropriately define the field.

One major exemplar working out of this post-Heideggerian trajectory is Hent de Vries. Through numerous volumes, he has elaborated
a sophisticated series of engagements with religion in contemporary
thought and political life. His pivotal work, *Philosophy and the Turn
to Religion* (1999), which draws heavily on the work of Jacques
Derrida, anticipates a great deal of the attention to religion subsequently generated in the wake of 9/11. It also illuminates well the
concerns underlying much recent work in continental philosophy of
religion. Unlike some scholars in continental philosophy of religion,
de Vries is deeply aware of recent work on the construction of the
category of religion. By the second page of the book he has invoked
both Jonathan Z. Smith and Talal Asad, and he explicitly rejects any
notion of religion as a natural category.[22] Nonetheless, his conception

---

Nonetheless, if Kant creates the opening, Heidegger typically figures as the one who
leads the way through it.

[22] See Hent de Vries, *Philosophy and the Turn to Religion* (Baltimore: Johns
Hopkins University Press, 1999), 1–2 and 8–9.

of philosophy's "turn to religion" is oriented by a notion of religion as a key site for the examination of alterity: "the formula *adieu* [a crucial Derridian conception for thinking about religion] accentuates the fact that every discourse, even the most secular, profane, negative, or nihilistic of utterances, directs and redirects itself unintentionally and unwittingly toward the alterity for which—historically, systematically, conceptually, and figuratively speaking—'God' is, perhaps and so far, the most proper name."[23] The latter part of the sentence makes clear that the notion of religion that occupies de Vries is one that associates God and alterity. This conjunction is not conceived in essentialist terms but is nonetheless presented as "historically, systematically, conceptually, and figuratively . . . most proper." Religion thus functions as the other of reason that incessantly interrupts and intrudes upon reason. At the same time, religion is implicated in the construction of reason, such that the two can never be fully separated. De Vries thus suggests an "alliance between the thought of difference and these often heterodox theological traditions" that are central to his consideration of religion.[24] As in the case of much work in analytic philosophy of religion, I see no reason to object to work on religion conceived in these terms. Nor should such work be ruled as not belonging in philosophy of religion. Nonetheless, to frame the inquiry in these terms directs philosophical attention away from the construction of these concepts themselves (as well as from many everyday experiences of religion on the ground). The notion of religion is chosen before the philosophical work itself begins.

More recently, however, de Vries has extended his engagement with the complexities surrounding the historical construction of the concept of religion. His edited volume, *Religion: Beyond a Concept* (2008), is the first volume in a series he also edits. The introduction to this volume, "Why Still 'Religion'?," wrestles with what he presents as the dual challenge of recognizing limits to any particular concept of religion (limits whose probing is part of the subject) and appreciating that thinking takes place via concepts, such that "*some* reference to *some* generic concept—here, 'religion'—is (and must be) kept in place for at least some time to come in even the most radical attempts to de-transcendentalize and naturalize its meaning

---

[23] De Vries, *Philosophy and the Turn*, 26.
[24] De Vries, *Philosophy and the Turn*, 38.

and use."[25] He does not abandon the concept but works against letting his object be fully grasped or contained by a concept. To do so, he seeks to build up from multitudinous particulars rather than strictly defining the boundaries of the topic in accord with any specific concept of religion: the project does not begin with that "arguably most difficult and, in the end, unanswerable—question 'What *is* "religion"?' Instead, the following essays and subsequent volumes prepare the ground for a more preliminary and hypothetical approach to the subject by asking what are the concrete and singular *vectors* from which the abstract question of 'religion' and its concept emerge."[26] Doing so opens the way to include engagement with a broader range of "words, things, gestures, powers, sounds, silences, smells, sensations, shapes, colors, affects, and effects."[27] The project thus supports the examination of, for instance, dimensions of lived religion left out of most work in philosophy of religion. Notably, I would argue that these formal claims about concept formation could be made of a range of other concepts, such as "liberalism." Religion is here, appropriately, being treated as one object of analysis among others, rather than conceived essentially in terms of reason's other before the investigation begins. (Admittedly, some passages in de Vries's introduction tend in the latter direction, but the overall direction of the project seems to frame the investigation without incorporating those presuppositions.[28]) Consequently, the orientation here offered to work in the philosophy of religion is promising—cognizant of the category's construction and open both to the study of this construction and to the philosophical examination of a wide range of materials historically associated with "religion." While the opening de Vries here offers is important, it also moves the broader project of this volume (and the series of which it forms the first book) beyond the scope of continental philosophy of religion. Many of the contributions to the volume fit in this category (continental philosophy of

---

[25] Hent de Vries, "Introduction: Why Still 'Religion'?," in *Religion: Beyond a Concept*, ed. Hent de Vries (New York: Fordham University Press, 2008), 2, emphasis in original.

[26] De Vries, "Introduction," 14, emphasis in original.

[27] De Vries, "Introduction," 14.

[28] For an example of this language, see "Introduction," 8: "A semantic black hole whose 'absence-presence' lets no single light escape, whether from its inner regions or from its surface . . . , 'religion' has resisted all enlightenment."

religion), but the introduction formulates the project in terms that can and should include more. In fact, with respect to my purposes here, the purview may be too broad: the framing just sketched is in no sense specific to the philosophy of religion but rather includes a plethora of studies of religion, taken up from a diverse range of perspectives (e.g., sociology, media studies, and history). In this respect, while de Vries's introductory framing moves beyond the limitations of much work in continental philosophy of religion and offers much that is promising for a broader conception of philosophy of religion, it does not in itself offer a program for philosophy of religion.

Reflecting back on these sketches of dominant directions in recent work in both analytic and continental philosophy of religion, it stands out that the vast majority of this scholarship has largely ignored the emphasis on sophisticated attention to history that has had such powerful effects in other subfields of religious studies. One major result of that lack of attention to history is insufficient cognizance of and engagement with the construction of the category of religion. Too much philosophy of religion still proceeds as if the concept of religion were sufficiently self-evident that one can largely ignore its construction.[29] For all their differences, analytic and continental philosophers of religion share in their relative non-engagement with the broader field of religious studies and its probing of this history. This lack of historical consciousness blinds us to our presuppositions and thereby deprives us of some of the most valuable resources for critique. More specifically, although the historicity of the concept of religion may be irrelevant for some questions, the lack of attention to one of the key concepts through which the field itself is defined renders it unnecessarily narrow and, in key respects, parochial. While excellent work can still be done within this frame, it is not hard to see why some

---

[29] These limitations also come out clearly in D. Z. Phillips and Timothy Tessin, eds., *Philosophy of Religion in the 21st Century* (Basingstoke; New York: Palgrave, 2001). While the work might seem dated as a portrayal of the field today, it is nonetheless revealing precisely because it seeks to incorporate analytic, continental, Wittgensteinian, and other approaches in order to give an overview of philosophy of religion as a whole. The reference to D. Z. Phillips will remind some that I have given remarkably little attention to another line of work in philosophy of religion—that inspired principally by Wittgenstein. Although by no means unimportant, this body of scholarship has not had nearly the influence of either analytic or continental philosophy of religion.

people view these discussions as profoundly shaped by unacknowledged Christian presuppositions and therefore not fully belonging in the academic study of religion.

The consequences of the narrowness of much work in philosophy of religion, however, extend well beyond the limitations to this work itself. The general lack of conversation between philosophers of religion, on one hand, and those probing the construction of the concept of religion and its consequences for the study of religion, on the other hand, has been bad for both sides. The field has benefited greatly from recent literature problematizing the history of the conceptualization of religion. Nonetheless—to speak in very broad terms—much of this material suffers from a flattened vision of modern Western religious thought inattentive to the depths and extent of debate in the West over just these issues (as in the understanding of ritual). In other words, this body of material suffers from too little conversation with philosophers of religion and scholars of religious thought.

PROMISING PROSPECTS

Something that is reasonably and justifiably called philosophy of religion has much more to offer the academic study of religion than the body of material just discussed. Such work not only contributes more broadly to the study of religion but also is informed by it. A number of recent works fit clearly into neither analytic nor continental philosophy of religion but engage both implicitly and explicitly with broader developments in religious studies, learning from as well as contributing to them. In doing so, despite their differences, such works illuminate vital pathways forward for the philosophy of religion.

To illustrate these possibilities, I turn briefly to three quite different examples: Amy Hollywood's *Sensible Ecstasy*, Jonathon Kahn's *Divine Discontent*, and Dan Arnold's *Brains, Buddhas, and Believing*. My discussions of these books are of a distinct sort: I focus here on the *kinds* of projects they offer and moves they make. The analysis, then, is in some sense formal. I do not try to summarize the entire books, to work through the particular claims they are making, or to judge the adequacy of their interpretations. By focusing instead on the forms of their projects as well as certain specific features, we can place in relief the models these represent for a new vision of philosophy of religion.

To be clear, I am not an expert in twentieth-century French thought, W. E. B. Du Bois, or classical Buddhist thought. I cannot speak to how responsibly these books engage with the primary or secondary materials or how they fit into other contemporary scholarship on these aspects of their topics. This caveat, however, is the flip side of precisely the kind of contribution that I want to highlight: despite their tremendous differences, all three of these works contribute to what I hope is an emerging discourse of philosophy of religion that exceeds the bounds that currently circumscribe most work done in the subfield. None of these books fit easily into the conversations of either "analytic philosophy of religion" or "continental philosophy of religion" as they usually proceed. All of them are philosophically oriented, theoretically sophisticated, and engaged with broad issues in the academic study of religion. Collectively, they provide diverse examples of what work in philosophy of religion that fully belongs in religious studies can and should be.[30]

Amy Hollywood's *Sensible Ecstasy: Mysticism, Sexual Difference, and the Demands of History* examines how a series of twentieth-century French theorists have taken up and engaged with medieval Christian women mystics. Framed by a broader concern with how we can acknowledge and respond to trauma and loss without making oppressed groups (particularly women) bear the burden of this process, the book focuses on Georges Bataille, Simone de Beauvoir, and Luce Irigaray to "trace this attraction to a feminized and embodied mystical figure and ask what work the figure of the medieval and early modern mystic performs, both epistemologically and affectively, for

---

[30] A number of other important recent examples of such work, on which I could also have focused here, include Matthew C. Bagger, *The Uses of Paradox: Religion, Self-Transformation, and the Absurd* (New York: Columbia University Press, 2007); Stephen S. Bush, *Visions of Religion: Experience, Meaning and Power* (Oxford: Oxford University Press, 2014); G. Scott Davis, *Believing and Acting: The Pragmatic Turn in Comparative Religion and Ethics* (Oxford: Oxford University Press, 2012); Andrew Dole, *Schleiermacher on Religion and the Natural Order* (Oxford: Oxford University Press, 2010); Sarah Hammerschlag, *The Figural Jew: Politics and Identity in Postwar French Thought* (Chicago: University of Chicago Press, 2010); Tyler T. Roberts, *Encountering Religion: Responsibility and Criticism after Secularism* (New York: Columbia University Press, 2013); and Kevin Schilbrack, *Philosophy and the Study of Religions: A Manifesto* (Malden, MA: Wiley Blackwell, 2014).

these secular, twentieth-century intellectuals."[31] Hollywood stresses that their treatments of mysticism concentrate on those forms associated with affect, emotion, and the body and frequently gendered as feminine. She interprets their engagements with this mysticism largely as efforts to express dimensions of human loss and suffering that press the limits of representation. For Hollywood, that work is both urgently necessary and frequently problematic, as she brings out in her treatments of the ethical and political dangers of several of these projects. While much of the book focuses on reading these modern French figures, she also brings to bear her own work on medieval mystics, frequently challenging what has been made of these women—by their contemporaries as well as in the twentieth century. In doing so, she ultimately takes up why these seemingly secular modern intellectuals turned to medieval Christian mystics, how they used them, and how they misread them—as well as how these mystics were construed in their own periods and what we should learn from all of these figures today.

The resulting project is extremely complex. It requires careful interrogation of the historical construction of key concepts, particularly mysticism. The probing of the gendering of more affective, embodied, and erotic forms of mysticism as feminine, for instance, culminates in the treatment of Beatrice of Nazareth (1200–1268) in chapter 8. Hollywood contrasts Beatrice's own "Seven Manners of Loving" with the portrayals of her offered by her male hagiographer. Hollywood concludes that the hagiographer frequently literalizes Beatrice's own bodily metaphors in a way that renders her mysticism more bodily than Beatrice's own accounts suggest.[32] By contrast, Beatrice's own account illustrates the emergence of forms of interiority that are typically associated with men of early modernity: "In forging this interiority, medieval women's texts are an important source for modern conceptions of the internalized self—conceptions that are currently under attack by many feminists."[33] Examining our accounts of the historical construction of key concepts thus funds revisions to our genealogies (in the broad, not necessarily Nietzschean or Foucaultian, sense) with significant normative implications.

---

[31] Hollywood, *Sensible Ecstasy*, 6.
[32] Hollywood, *Sensible Ecstasy*, 247–66.
[33] Hollywood, *Sensible Ecstasy*, 265.

Moreover, Hollywood consistently interrogates these constructions with a keen eye for their political stakes and operations. In the case of Beatrice, for instance, Hollywood not only convincingly argues that the hagiography "tends to represent internal dispositions of the soul through external narrative devices," such that her body becomes "the visible site of her sanctity."[34] She also connects the hagiographer's emphasis on the body to conflict between Catholic authorities and the Cathars, a conflict that was itself "crucially centered on issues of materiality and embodiment."[35] Attention to the political context thus does significant work in explaining how women's mysticism came to be associated with the body more than interiority.

While Hollywood engages explicitly with the construction of notions of mysticism, her concern with the category "religion" is more subtle, though still significant. She frames the inquiry in terms of why a group of "resolutely secular, even anti-Christian intellectuals" would turn to Christian mystics but devotes relatively little energy to conceptualizing religion, Christianity, or secularity.[36] Instead, she pushes against boundaries to the categories and demonstrates what can be gained by transgressing what some see as a crucial boundary. From the beginning, her engagement with the nexus of mysticism and feminism moves back and forth across what is often taken to be a strong boundary between religious and secular thought. In her reading of Sartre's critique of Bataille, for instance, she demonstrates what is lost if we fail to appreciate the way that categories such as atheism and theism are being contested.[37] In doing so, she shows that the study of figures viewed as paradigmatically religious has much to contribute to inquiries that are not and, conversely, that engagement with figures generally treated as firmly within "the Christian tradition" cannot afford to ignore what goes on outside this ostensible tradition. More pointedly, she illuminates the limits of the category of religion even when examining topics typically conceived as paradigmatically religious, such as mysticism.

This attention to the history of categories is closely tied to a broader attention to history. In a manner that distinguishes her work from the majority of religious studies scholarship dealing with ideas, Hollywood repeatedly locates texts and figures in thickly textured portrayals of their intellectual, social, and political contexts.

---

[34] Hollywood, *Sensible Ecstasy*, 252.   [35] Hollywood, *Sensible Ecstasy*, 254.
[36] Hollywood, *Sensible Ecstasy*, 6.   [37] Hollywood, *Sensible Ecstasy*, 35.

Whether dealing with the impact of the Second World War on Bataille's treatment of suffering, the impact of French student protests in May 1968 on Kristeva's circle, or the significance of conflict with Cathars for Beatrice's hagiography, Hollywood illuminates the costs of attempting to treat ideas without attending to the contexts in which they emerged or reemerged.[38]

Beyond this careful reading of texts and attention to history, *Sensible Ecstasy* is explicit about its own normative claims. It does much more than ask why twentieth-century theorists have been drawn to these mystics: it makes constructive claims about pleasure, loss, the limits of representation, and the construction of subjectivity through engagement with both medieval Christian women mystics and modern authors who engage this legacy.[39] On the basis of this engagement, she argues for the importance of developing ways to acknowledge loss and its embodiment without associating the body exclusively with suffering rather than pleasure. Successful strategies for doing so will need to avoid the gender binary structuring much of Kristeva's thought and to recognize the limits of politics for avoiding loss altogether. Loss and trauma are inevitable—which is not to say we should not do what we can to limit and lessen them—and we need expressive forms and even rituals to acknowledge them. Hollywood concurs with the secular French intellectuals she examines that medieval Christian mystics provide valuable sources for probing these issues. In our turning to them, however, we need to be wary of dangerous forms of irrationalism that frequently arise in such returns. Crucially, much of the insight is generated by reading the bodies of texts together as well as in relation to their own historical settings. The book thus represents an admirable convergence of interpretive, historical, and constructive work.

Finally, the precision of the prose merits mention for what it enables the book to do. Hollywood develops nuanced readings of extraordinarily challenging texts. Moreover, several of these texts conceive themselves as challenging claims to the transparency of language. They probe the limits of representation. Hollywood does not play down or ignore these aspects of their projects. In the case of

---

[38] Hollywood, *Sensible Ecstasy*, 25, 32, 60–2, 136, 176, and 253–5.

[39] These connections are most obvious in chapter 8 and the conclusion, but they are present throughout the book. See, for instance, her discussion of Bataille's use of photographs of victims of torture (90–5).

Bataille, for instance, she takes seriously his intention to engender particular experiences in the reader rather than to set out a pellucid system or program. Nonetheless, she does so with language that aspires to, and usually achieves, remarkable clarity and precision. In doing so, she brings these figures into a broader conversation that is not undermined by claims of ineffability or conversation-stopping appeals to experience.

Jonathon Kahn's *Divine Discontent: The Religious Imagination of W. E. B. Du Bois* argues that Du Bois is best understood as developing a form of pragmatic religious naturalism. An adequate understanding of Du Bois's thought—not simply his religious thought, but his project more generally—requires appreciating both his critiques of religion and its ongoing significance for him. This ongoing significance consists not in a kind of hidden Christianity, nor simply in a penchant for religious imagery. To the contrary, Kahn situates Du Bois in the tradition of pragmatic religious naturalism that he initially associates with William James, George Santayana, and John Dewey (and he provides a very lucid account of their projects as elaborating forms of religious naturalism). The notion of pragmatic religious naturalism thus enables Kahn to do justice to the depth and significance of Du Bois's engagement with his religious heritage without simply interpreting him as a crypto-Christian. For Kahn:

> Pragmatic religious naturalists subvert traditional religious metaphysics of ultimate truth and foundational beliefs while holding tight to religious stories, moods, symbols, rhetoric, and moral values because they are links to the past, because they are powerful tools for shaping and envisioning life, and because they can allow for a type of spirituality that emphasizes the fallibility, fragility, and power of the human-made ties that bind us and make us dependent on each other.... Pragmatic religious naturalists conceive of religion as funding the deepest sources of ourselves, while insisting that those sources get their depth from linguistic and historical webs of meaning.[40]

Note the extent of contrast with the conceptions of religion operating in much work in analytic philosophy of religion. Precisely by engaging with a broader range of work in the study of religion, Kahn brings to his materials a more sophisticated and nuanced understanding of religion's potential significance.

---

[40] Kahn, *Divine Discontent*, 13.

Doing so illuminates dimensions of Du Bois's thought that otherwise remain obscure, such as his extensive treatments of sacrifice and lynching parables. Du Bois participates in a long tradition of African American thought associating lynching with the crucifixion, yet he does so without justifying or sanctifying this suffering and death.[41] In drawing attention to the subtlety of Du Bois's engagement with the traditions he inherits, Kahn simultaneously explains why scholars with narrower conceptions of religion (who may see only the rejection of the sanctification of this suffering) easily read him as rejecting religion altogether. Moreover, this attention to pragmatic religious naturalism enables Kahn to demonstrate what Du Bois adds to this tradition. That is, the broader context of pragmatic religious naturalism does not reduce Du Bois to a derivation of the classic, white American pragmatists. Rather, it provides the context that allows us to appreciate the way that he advances this tradition by bringing it together with the history of African American religious thought.

Kahn's treatment of Du Bois's pragmatic religious naturalism is pervasively concerned with matters of ethics. His elaboration of Du Bois's religious naturalism is occupied with the virtues that are central to it. In particular, Kahn develops Du Bois's account of how we relate to the sources of our present in terms of the virtue of piety. Here again, one goes easily astray if one limits the conception of piety to models provided by figures such as Augustine and Friedrich Schleiermacher. Crucial to Kahn's interpretation of piety is a more democratically inflected notion that nonetheless needs to be interpreted in relation to a particular history of thinking about how we relate to our sources and history.[42] Kahn's focus on piety as a virtue is important because it is emblematic of the way that important recent work is productively blurring the divide that has often separated work in religious ethics from much other work in philosophy of religion. In this case, we cannot understand Du Bois's contribution to philosophy of religion if we fail to see his ethics as integral thereto.

In my reading, much of the power of Kahn's book to contribute to a range of broader discussions derives from his explicit engagement with the conceptualization of religion. It is precisely because he moves beyond the particular notions of religion prominent in both analytic and continental philosophy of religion that he can demonstrate the

---

[41] Kahn, *Divine Discontent*, 122–3.
[42] Kahn, *Divine Discontent*, 71–81.

importance of religion for interpreting Du Bois. Further, showing religion's significance for a figure such as Du Bois, who is so often interpreted as simply hostile to religion, opens up new pathways to appreciate the importance of attending to religion in a wide range of figures, movements, and lives that are often portrayed in exclusively secular terms. Studies of this sort are invaluable in showing how the study of religion offers tools vital to the interpretation and critique of so many aspects of our contemporary world—even those where religion is ostensibly absent. Moreover, it is precisely the philosophical aspects of Kahn's project that make this contribution possible.

Dan Arnold's most recent book, *Brains, Buddhas, and Believing: The Problem of Intentionality in Classical Buddhist and Cognitive-Scientific Philosophy of Mind*, takes up central issues in philosophical debates over the kinds of explanations that can be given for thought. Specifically, is it possible to explain thought in terms of causes and effects? Much of the analysis focuses on the seventh-century Indian Buddhist thinker Dharmakīrti, but Dharmakīrti is brought into fruitful conversation with other first-millennium Indian thinkers (both Brahmanical and Buddhist) as well as with modern Western thinkers—particularly Immanuel Kant, Jerry Fodor, Wilfrid Sellars, and John McDowell. Arnold concludes that the same kinds of arguments against physicalism that he views as undermining Fodor's position (and consequently much recent work in cognitive science) also damage Dharmakīrti's very different account of the mental. In both cases, the decisive problem lies in the effort to provide causal explanations of thought. The result simultaneously offers impressive exegesis of first-millennium South Asian as well as recent Western thought, exemplifies excellence in comparative study, explicitly interweaves exegetical and normative aspects of the project, and examines the wide-ranging implications for contemporary work in philosophy of mind, cognitive science, and method and theory in the study of religion.

In my reading, the work is exemplary in its attempt to bring thinkers from very different times and places into a common conversation without sacrificing analytic precision or attention to intellectual contexts. Thus, even though the book focuses on Dharmakīrti, it is comparative in the best sense. Crucially, the book does not simply compare and contrast early Indian views with modern Western views. It argues powerfully that figures in both contexts were disagreeing over closely related issues: on what he takes to be the decisive questions regarding explanations of thought, Dharmakīrti, Jerry

Fodor, and Ilkka Pyysiäinen can be lined up on one side and (Brahmanical) Mīmāṃsaka and (Buddhist) Mādhyamika thinkers as well as Kant, Sellars, and McDowell on the other. In making this claim, Arnold by no means suggests that the thinkers on each side of this divide are all saying the same thing. Rather, his analysis emphasizes the extent of their differences. Much of the book's work consists in developing subtle, context-sensitive arguments that—amidst these differences—one can discern fundamental commonalities on each side regarding whether, as he puts it in the conclusion, "insofar as the project of 'naturalizing' intentionality consists in advancing essentially causal explanations of the contentful character of thought, there is something about intentionality that *cannot* be accounted for thereby."[43] To be sure, making this case involves a great deal of careful exegetical work and is only successful to the extent that the interpretive claims are sensitive to the thinker's work as a whole.

Importantly, recent Western philosophers do not simply provide the analytical concepts through which "others" are analyzed, such that those from the modern West present a purportedly neutral framework or vocabulary against which the thought of others is implicitly or explicitly measured. To the contrary, Arnold's examination of the early Indian thinkers is conceived to make critical interventions in ongoing Western conversations, not simply to enlighten the former with the purportedly neutral clarity of the latter. Mīmāṃsaka and Mādhyamika thinkers are thus presented as offering compelling objections to Fodor's project, not only to Dharmakīrti's; and Arnold contends that the fact that their arguments (as well as Kant's and McDowell's) pertain to Fodor (as well as to Dharmakīrti) teaches us a great deal about what matters are actually at issue. Thus, the light shed by comparison shines in both directions: "some first-millennium Indian philosophers can help us understand the nature and limits of some eminently twenty-first century developments in philosophy of mind," just as much as the contrary.[44]

To make these connections powerful and convincing, Arnold has to pay close attention to the larger intellectual contexts in which the thinkers operated. His manner of attending to context, however, contrasts importantly with Hollywood's. While Arnold occasionally notes particular political considerations, he tends to minimize these

---

[43] Arnold, *Brains, Buddhas, and Believing*, 236, emphasis in original.
[44] Arnold, *Brains, Buddhas, and Believing*, 18.

to focus on a narrower set of philosophical concerns. For instance, Arnold notes multiple motivations Dharmakīrti would have for critiquing Brahmanical views of language as eternal: "Ideologically speaking, Buddhists were surely concerned to undermine the authoritative status of the Vedic corpus that provides the basis for Brahmanical social formations." After linking the critique of such Brahmanical claims to the kind of analysis developed by theorists such as Pierre Bourdieu, Arnold continues: "In this light, Buddhist arguments for the contingent character of language surely reflect a concern to deflate Brahmanical status by developing, as Sheldon Pollock says, 'a wider-ranging understanding of contingency or conventionalism in human life'. . . . " Noting these "ideological" motives, however, Arnold moves quickly on: "While Buddhists surely aimed to advance such concerns by elaborating the *apoha* [exclusion] doctrine, what is of interest for us is the philosophical issues motivating the doctrine."[45] Arnold does not deny political motives, but he focuses on what he presents as the properly "philosophical" issues. While I take Hollywood to make a powerful case that "philosophical" issues cannot be separated from political concerns as neatly as Arnold's language suggests, Arnold's work demonstrates the results that are also possible with a narrower focus. With those fruits in mind, I think it would be a mistake to insist that all work in philosophy of religion must engage with political contexts and stakes to the degree that Hollywood does.

For Arnold, the attention to context consists first and foremost in locating particular arguments within the thinker's larger intellectual positions, as he illustrates at virtually every step in his analysis. As part of this attention, Arnold notes at important points the roles that broader religious commitments play. Here in particular we see what Arnold, as a philosopher of religion, offers that goes beyond what could be achieved by a philosophical analysis that paid no attention to religion. After noting the parallels between Dharmakīrti's focus on causality and the empiricism of figures such as John Locke, Arnold notes that Dharmakīrti's manner of combining emphases on causality and mental dispositions "fits well with central Buddhist commitments." Thus, "the connection . . . between causal description and the subjective is part of the deep grammar of the Buddhist tradition."[46] Claims such as these both situate the particular arguments in a broader

---

[45] Arnold, *Brains, Buddhas, and Believing*, 119–20.
[46] Arnold, *Brains, Buddhas, and Believing*, 30, 31.

Buddhist context and—by doing so—connect the theoretical issues at the center of Arnold's book to central debates in the history of Buddhist thought. We can make such a point, I believe, even while harboring skepticism about the notion of a "deep grammar of [a] tradition." Arnold's work thus illustrates that moving philosophy of religion beyond a focus principally on Christianity will also make new topics—such as accounts of intentionality—integral to philosophy of religion. It will move us beyond questions generated largely by the history of Christian thought and practice to encompass those emerging from other religious contexts as well.

Identifying the connections between particular claims and what some would identify as important tenets of Buddhism, however, does not replace or obviate the need for argument—for Dharmakīrti or for Arnold. This point comes out in the role in Dharmakīrti's argument of "the thought that the Buddha exemplified a fathomlessly profound degree of compassion . . . ."[47] According to Arnold, this commitment serves as the starting point for a kind of transcendental argument:

> That this thought should occasion the elaboration, in the remainder of the chapter, of a comprehensive defense of a Buddhist worldview nicely exemplifies, I think, what it is to do philosophy. What Dharmakīrti effectively does, in the remainder of the chapter, is systematically consider *what else must be true* for his thought to make sense—and to think philosophically about one's commitments just is to reflect carefully on what else one is committed to in virtue of believing anything.[48]

This vision of the practice of philosophy as the analysis of what is entailed by a given commitment usefully describes a great deal of the philosophical reflection that takes place in the context of religion. Importantly, in a footnote immediately preceding this quote, Arnold suggests the accord between this use of reasoned analysis and Dharmakīrti's own conception of inquiry: Dharmakīrti is himself concerned to avoid allowing "the testimony of a tradition" itself to function as a given in the argument.[49] Arnold thus demonstrates that this conception of philosophical inquiry need not be conceived in fundamental opposition to "religion" itself; we need not understand religion as intrinsically antithetical to reason. Phrases such as

---

[47] Arnold, *Brains, Buddhas, and Believing,* 31.
[48] Arnold, *Brains, Buddhas, and Believing,* 32.
[49] Arnold, *Brains, Buddhas, and Believing,* 251 n. 41.

"taking religion seriously," then, should not entail treating claims in the context of religion as givens; doing so treats them as conversation stoppers in a manner at odds with their functions in most discussions among religious figures. While Arnold might do more than he does to question whether what he views as the problematic implications of Dharmakīrti's premise (at least as Dharmakīrti works them out) might be taken to count against the premise, he nonetheless models important ways in which philosophical analysis bears on the study of religion. Appreciating this model does not commit us to accepting this vision as the entirety of philosophy of religion (as an over-reading of the above passage could suggest) but powerfully portrays a vital option.

In combining attention to claims often seen as central to Buddhism with arguments that these positions (whether Dharmakīrti's or Fodor's) are intellectually indefensible, Arnold not only offers transparency regarding his normative claims but also avoids presenting these as somehow threatening or even undermining "Buddhism." That is, Arnold's recurrent attention to debates *among* Buddhists over just the issues he is examining—as in Nāgārjuna's critiques of Dharmakīrti—makes clear that his critiques of Dharmakīrti's positions do not count against Buddhism or the idea of selflessness as such.[50] Arnold's treatment thus represents an important step beyond comparative analyses that treat entities such as "Buddhism," "Islam," or "Christianity" as effective units of analysis.

In the final pages of the book, Arnold returns explicitly to the study's significance for the broader field of religious studies—bridging precisely the chasm that I have argued needs bridging. He first takes up recent work in cognitive science of religion such as that of Ilkka Pyysiäinen. Building on central elements of his larger argument, Arnold highlights the way that the arguments he has developed (through engagement with Dharmakīrti and many others) against "purportively exhaustive causal accounts of the mental" cut at fundamental assumptions of much work in cognitive science of religion.[51] The conclusions he articulates here follow closely from the central arguments through the book as a whole. Arnold briefly demonstrates that even Pyysiäinen, who seems more engaged with the broader field of religious studies than most cognitive scientists of

---

[50] Arnold, *Brains, Buddhas, and Believing*, 238.
[51] Arnold, *Brains, Buddhas, and Believing*, 236, 240–1.

religion, is vulnerable to the criticisms of efficient-causal explanations of thought developed over the course of the book.[52] In doing so, Arnold concisely but powerfully demonstrates philosophy of religion's significance for the now widespread interest in cognitive science of religion.

Having dispensed with the cognitive science of religion, Arnold turns to another influential body of recent literature in religious studies: the work of Talal Asad as well as of the new materialism associated with Mark Taylor's *Critical Terms for Religious Studies*.[53] Arnold lauds the focus on more than doctrine and belief. Nonetheless, he provocatively argues that this current in the field—in its denigration of the significance of belief—shares with the cognitive scientists the view that we can—and should—do without "*an intentional level of description*."[54] Much of this body of work, then, is vulnerable to the arguments developed throughout Arnold's book. One might question, however, whether Arnold here attributes to his opponents a more elaborated philosophy of mind than is warranted. While certain presuppositions operative in Asad, for instance, do seem to stand at odds with Arnold's position, their underdevelopment in Asad's work makes it difficult to judge precisely how much of Asad's position is undermined by the charge. For we have here returned to precisely the body of literature with which my Introduction began: thinkers such as Asad, Masuzawa, and Catherine Bell, who have done so much to shape dominant discourse in the field of religious studies over the last two decades. And as valuable as this material has been, the lack of more extensive engagement with the concerns central to Arnold's book reveals the costs of so little interaction between these scholars and philosophers of religion. We need more sustained attention to the underlying philosophical assumptions operative in work on method in religious studies.

---

[52] Arnold, *Brains, Buddhas, and Believing*, 240–1.

[53] See Talal Asad, *Genealogies of Religion: Discipline and Reasons of Power in Christianity and Islam* (Baltimore: Johns Hopkins University Press, 1993); Talal Asad, *Formations of the Secular: Christianity, Islam, Modernity* (Stanford: Stanford University Press, 2003); Mark C. Taylor, ed., *Critical Terms for Religious Studies* (Chicago: University of Chicago Press, 1998).

[54] Arnold, *Brains, Buddhas, and Believing*, 242. Arnold's treatment is largely shaped by Terry Godlove's now classic essay, Terry F. Godlove, Jr., "Saving Belief: On the New Materialism in Religious Studies," in *Radical Interpretation in Religion*, ed. Nancy K. Frankenberry (Cambridge: Cambridge University Press, 2002), 10–24.

Across their differences, the books of Hollywood, Kahn, and Arnold suggest an expansive vision of philosophy of religion that overcomes the limitations characterizing much work in the field today. They move beyond a dominant focus on Christianity not simply with respect to the materials they examine but also in terms of the questions they bring to bear—whether these questions are generated by the materials being examined or the process of examination itself. These questions frequently demonstrate the artificiality of separating ethics from other dimensions of philosophy of religion. These books thus regularly straddle the divide that has often been constructed between philosophy of religion and religious ethics, demonstrating that the deepest issues at stake in each belong no less to the other. The works also expand the range of genres examined, treating poetry and fiction as well as more traditional theological and philosophical prose.

Perhaps more fundamentally, these books probe, both implicitly and explicitly, the conceptualization of religion. They frequently transgress the boundaries of the more everyday conceptions of religion operating in much philosophy of religion, and they show the value of doing so for illuminating the thought of seemingly secular figures such as Bataille and Du Bois. They illustrate not only an enriched conception of philosophy of religion but also the vital contributions of the study of religion to figures who are often treated without attention to religion. All three of these works display a fine-grained attention to history. Their attention to history—to figures from the past richly embedded in their intellectual, social, and political contexts—coheres closely with their attention to the construction of key categories. Moreover, each of these works demonstrates that carefully elaborated critical readings of others' texts can contribute to—rather than simply compete with—the development of the authors' own normative claims.

Collectively, then, works such as these suggest promising prospects for the field of philosophy of religion. They illustrate well a vision of the field not principally as the philosophical analysis of classic questions regarding the rationality of theism and its consequences but as an inclusive deployment of philosophical modes of analysis in the study of religion. Philosophy of religion so conceived attends to diverse religions and materials and to the construction of central concepts of the analysis. It is explicitly normatively engaged while also being historically informed and sensitive.

2

On the Role of Normativity in Religious Studies

Like other fields across the humanities and social sciences, religious studies grapples with the complex and often hidden relationships between descriptions and normative presuppositions and implications—roughly, between claims about what is and about what ought to be. For reasons concerning both its subject matter and the history of the field, however, debates about these issues in religious studies are both particularly charged and particularly illuminating. Here, the issues have largely arisen in the context of debates over the appropriate substance, methods, and approaches in the academic study of religion. These debates, in turn, have often been framed in terms of the relation between religious studies and theology. Critics have repeatedly charged that the field remains tainted, that it has not yet escaped the die cast by its largely Protestant theological roots. For these critics, the field thus functions as a kind of liberal Protestant—or, at best, ecumenical—apologetics. Where earlier debates were concerned with obviously theological work being done in religious studies, recent scholarship has highlighted the more subtle endurance of broadly Protestant presuppositions even in supposedly more pluralistic conceptions of the study of religion.[1] From the other side, theologians decry an exclusion that

---

[1] See, for example, Timothy Fitzgerald, *The Ideology of Religious Studies* (Oxford: Oxford University Press, 2000); Jonathan Z. Smith, *Drudgery Divine: On the Comparison of Early Christianities and the Religions of Late Antiquity* (Chicago: University of Chicago Press, 1990); Daniel Dubuisson, *The Western Construction of Religion: Myths, Knowledge, and Ideology*, trans. William Sayers (Baltimore: Johns Hopkins University Press, 2003); Tomoko Masuzawa, *The Invention of World Religions, Or, How European Universalism Was Preserved in the Language of Pluralism* (Chicago:

they see as based in no-longer defensible models of objectivity and rationality. Some of these theologians seek to transmute postmodern critiques of reason into tickets for readmission to the guild.[2]

In much of this debate, a crucial background assumption— sometimes stated but often not—is that whereas theologians make normative claims, religious studies scholars should refrain from doing so. Rather, scholars in religious studies should distinguish themselves from theologians precisely by striving for some type of distance, neutrality, or objectivity in relation to their subject matter, where this is understood to entail analysis regarding what is rather than claims about what ought to be. The account of this relationship might be formulated in a variety of ways, some more modern, some with a postmodern aspect. At times, those who do normative work are contrasted with historians, who are presumably investigating an object with a degree of openness to the data and a determination to abstain from judging that is seen as lacking in the normative thinker. In other cases, the "normative" work of theologians is contrasted with the "analysis" that should distinguish religious studies.[3]

In considering this debate, it bears noticing that work in a number of other disciplines regularly makes explicitly normative claims without arousing suspicion that it does not belong. Philosophy and political science provide some of the most obvious examples. Apparently, explicitly normative claims associated with religion provoke greater suspicion than normative claims in other areas. This inequality of suspicion, I want to suggest, points us toward hidden assumptions largely responsible for the intractability of this debate. Normativity is

University of Chicago Press, 2005); and Russell T. McCutcheon, *Critics Not Caretakers: Redescribing the Public Study of Religion* (Albany: State University of New York Press, 2001).

[2] Variations of this strategy are a recurrent motif in the March 2006 *Journal of the American Academy of Religion* on the theme, "The Future of the Study of Religion in the Academy." See, for instance, Ellen T. Armour, "Theology in Modernity's Wake," *Journal of the American Academy of Religion* 74, no. 1 (2006): 7–10, and Gavin Flood, "Reflections on Tradition and Inquiry in the Study of Religions," *Journal of the American Academy of Religion* 74, no. 1 (2006): 48. Robert Orsi notes this broader tendency as well; Robert A. Orsi, *Between Heaven and Earth: The Religious Worlds People Make and the Scholars Who Study Them* (Princeton: Princeton University Press, 2005), 194.

[3] Orsi's use of "normative" in Orsi, *Between Heaven and Earth*, chapter 6, sometimes carries the former sense. McCutcheon's language often contrasts the "analysis" that he sees as appropriate to religious studies with the "normative" claims that are not (e.g., McCutcheon, *Critics Not Caretakers*, 134–5).

viewed differently in relation to religion because of a pervasive assumption that religion cannot be argued about—that it is, in essence, "reason's other." In this view of religion, normative claims related to religion cannot be argued about but are fundamentally matters of "faith." This I take to be the most problematic theological presupposition that continues to haunt discussions of religion—a presupposition shared by many writers on both sides of the debate.

More precisely put, the drive to define religious studies largely through the contrast with theology too often rests on two closely related, highly problematic presuppositions: first, of those writing on religion, only the theologians make normative claims and, second, normative claims related to religion are fundamentally a matter of faith, where faith is juxtaposed with reason. While the latter supposition is undoubtedly valid for many normative religious claims that are made, it is not valid for all. As we think about how to construct the discipline of religious studies, it is essential that we not build this presupposition into its foundations. We should not exclude such views, but neither should they be fundamental to the conception of the discipline.

With these concerns in mind, I want to argue that our discussions about the distinctiveness of the academic study of religion should be recast from debates about religious studies v. theology or descriptive v. normative work to a focus on normativity and the justification of normative claims. My point is not to include every kind of writing on "religion" as appropriate for religious studies but to reframe the discussion in order to provide more defensible and coherent criteria for inclusion or exclusion. Let me stress that the concern here is with the boundaries of religious studies, not the particular approaches I find most convincing; there are of course many approaches that I find unproductive or based on mistakes that I nonetheless do not want to exclude from the discipline. Framing the debate in terms of theology and religious studies, however, is ultimately neither intellectually defensible nor heuristically productive. The term "theology" covers too much that is too diverse in crucial respects; it occludes by eliding differences. Shifting the frame should help to dissolve a number of pseudo-arguments and illuminate the substantive intellectual issues, issues that are shared with many disciplines across the university.

Focusing on the issue of normativity, I want to begin with a rather simple claim: Normative claims are inevitable in the study of religion (as in most if not all disciplines). What is important is not to try somehow to exclude normative claims but rather to be willing to offer justification for the norms that we invoke. Participants in the academic study of religion must be willing to bring the norms themselves into debate and subject them to critical inquiry. The shift of attention I propose, then, is ultimately to the justification offered for particular norms. The moves that exclude one from the discipline are appeals to an authority that is claimed not to require justification, appeals to an authority conceived as unquestionable, and appeals to private forms of justification for which, in principle, no argument can be given.

THE INEVITABILITY OF NORMATIVITY

In speaking of normativity, I have in mind claims—whether made explicit or remaining implicit—regarding the way we ought to act or think. In describing ethical claims as "normative," Christine Korsgaard writes, "They make *claims* on us; they command, oblige, recommend, or guide. Or at least, when we invoke them, we make claims on one another. . . . Concepts like knowledge, beauty, and meaning, as well as virtue and justice, all have a normative dimension, for they tell us what to think, what to like, what to say, what to do, and what to be."[4] Focusing on the breadth of the term, Jonathan Dancy writes, "our 'ought' here is not particularly a moral ought, nor even just a practical ought. . . . For the notion of value (good and bad) is held to be as normative as the notion of the right."[5] Normativity need not be limited to deontological conceptions of morality, in which the central ethical issue concerns the choices we make and these are evaluated in terms of adherence to a formal moral norm rather than their results. Rather, normativity as a whole concerns a wider range of judgments of value. It is in play any time judgments of value are made, whether implicitly or explicitly.

---

[4] Christine Korsgaard, *The Sources of Normativity* (Cambridge: Cambridge University Press, 1996), 8–9.

[5] Jonathan Dancy, "Editor's Introduction," in *Normativity*, ed. Jonathan Dancy (Oxford: Blackwell Publishers, 2000), vii. For a similar focus on "ought," see Ralph Wedgwood, *The Nature of Normativity* (Oxford: Clarendon Press, 2007), 1.

Attending to the broad scope of normativity will enable us to appreciate its role even in empirical research where it is least suspected. With regard to the subject at hand, this attention to judgments of value is particularly relevant: it simultaneously points to what many have objected to in the work of scholars defending a particular tradition over others and enables us to identify normative claims made by many of the most vocal critics of the role theology has played in the field. Conceiving of normativity broadly in this manner in itself leaves a great deal open regarding the different ways in which norms are understood to be grounded.

As broad as this conception is, however, I do want to focus on normative judgments of the materials or people a scholar studies. It is *also* the case that scholars presuppose norms for scholarship itself. In fact, it is precisely these norms that we are debating. But the point here is that in addition to presupposing or defending norms for the practice of academic work itself, scholars also inevitably make normative judgments regarding the materials and people they are studying. One could also treat views on what counts as a good justification in terms of epistemic normativity, but I am making a more focused claim about normative value judgments of the subjects being studied.

For the present purposes, a few relevant examples will be more helpful than further theorizing of the concept of normativity.[6] In order to make the case as persuasive as possible, I have chosen representative examples spanning a range of approaches, some of which are among those that seem least likely to be normative. The most obvious examples of normative claims are those that explicitly invoke the language of "should" or "ought." Kant's categorical imperative, "act only in accordance with that maxim through which you can at the same time will that it become a universal law," provides a classic example.[7] Much scholarship in ethics—whether philosophical or religious—falls

---

[6] For a concise treatment of important philosophical discussions of the relation between description and normativity, see Hilary Putnam, "Objectivity and the Science-Ethics Distinction," in *The Quality of Life*, ed. Martha C. Nussbaum and Amartya Sen (Oxford: Clarendon Press, 1993), 143–57. For an important recent contribution to this still lively philosophical debate, see Robert Brandom, *Between Saying and Doing: Towards an Analytic Pragmatism* (Oxford: Oxford University Press, 2008).

[7] Immanuel Kant, *Groundwork of the Metaphysics of Morals*, in *Practical Philosophy*, ed. Mary J. Gregor and Allen W. Wood and trans. Mary J. Gregor, The Cambridge Edition of the Works of Immanuel Kant (Cambridge: Cambridge University Press, 1999), 73.

into this category, as in arguments about the morality of abortion, the war in Iraq, or social justice.

Although such claims might be explicitly religious, they need not be. Drawing on Aristotle, the philosopher Martha Nussbaum argues that we can identify "sphere[s] of universal experience and choice," such as "bodily appetites and their pleasures," "distribution of limited resources," and so forth.[8] In each of these spheres, human beings are necessarily faced with choices about how to act: "If it is not appropriate, it is inappropriate; it cannot be off the map altogether. People will of course disagree about what the appropriate ways of acting and reacting in fact *are*. But in that case, as Aristotle has set things up, they are arguing about the same thing, and advancing competing specifications of the same virtue."[9] The virtues, such as moderation and justice, are simply ways of talking about what it is to choose appropriately in each sphere. Nussbaum is concerned here to highlight the way that this approach frames the issues so that competing ethical views can be understood as competing arguments about a common topic; but that point should not let us lose sight of the normative force of the competing specifications of each virtue—the kind of specification that Nussbaum engages in greater detail in other parts of her corpus.[10] Significantly, though she is explicitly normative, her being so does not raise questions about whether she belongs in a secular university.

Though these works in ethics are obviously normative, other projects reveal these not to be a special case. We are also making normative claims when we interpret a particular religious practice as an expression of a universal human need—for community or solidarity, for instance. Such theories typically, if often implicitly, make the satisfaction of such needs normative for human beings. Value is attributed to the practice by virtue of its satisfaction of this need.

Take, for example, the work of the historian of religion, Robert Orsi. Orsi has been deeply concerned with how religion should be studied academically and with the ongoing influence of Protestant

---

[8] Martha C. Nussbaum, "Non-Relative Virtues: An Aristotelian Approach," in Nussbaum and Sen, *The Quality of Life*, 246. Although Martha Nussbaum currently holds appointments in the University of Chicago Law School, the Philosophy Department, and the Divinity School, I identify her principally as a philosopher.

[9] Nussbaum, "Non-Relative Virtues," 247.

[10] See, for instance, Martha C. Nussbaum, *Women and Human Development: The Capabilities Approach* (Cambridge: Cambridge University Press, 2000), especially chapter 1.

theology on the field. Even he, however, makes important normative claims. One example comes from his *Between Heaven and Earth*. The background for this passage is his research for his earlier book, *Thank You, St. Jude*, on devotion to the patron saint of hopeless causes. One of the women he interviewed had asked him whether he had ever prayed to St. Jude. At a later point, he did not exactly pray to St. Jude but he did something that he viewed as comparable: "Instead of actually praying to Saint Jude I tried to find some analogue to this act in my own emotional and behavioral repertoire."[11] As a result of this experience and its impact on him, he writes, "what I learned as I tried to take Clara's challenge seriously is that we were alike none-theless in our need, vulnerability, and risk."[12] Here, Orsi is claiming a "common humanity," characterized by need and vulnerability, and discussing the value of a variety of responses to this human predica-ment. Crucially, his understanding of Clara's action in these terms (with the normative claims entailed) determines his characterization of her action. More generally, any time we claim—explicitly or implicitly—that human behavior can be explained in a particular way—as the pursuit of economic interests or cultural capital, for instance—we are making controversial claims about the nature of human existence with important consequences for how we should live. And as Orsi's example indicates, even a scholar who rejects strongly reductionist accounts of religion will invoke normative claims as soon as he or she moves past the most superficial levels of description. Even the question of what merits explanation—e.g., men possessing more power than women in a given society—depends in part on normative commitments. These claims too, then, are normative.

Lest the normativity in the above example be attributed to apolo-getics on Orsi's part, however, it will be helpful to consider scholars even more critical of their subjects' self-understanding. Timothy Fitzgerald is an ardent critic of the discipline of religious studies, largely on the grounds of the pervasiveness of an "ecumenical liberal theology [that] has been disguised (though not very well) in the so-called scientific study of religion." In *The Ideology of Religious Studies*, he seeks to expose the way in which the resulting conception of "religion" as a generic concept has not only corrupted much—though by no means all—of the work done in the field but also underwritten

---

[11] Orsi, *Between Heaven and Earth*, 172.
[12] Orsi, *Between Heaven and Earth*, 173.

major political projects: "The construction of 'religion' and 'religions' as global, crosscultural objects of study has been part of a wider historical process of western imperialism, colonialism, and neocolonialism. Part of this process has been to establish an ideologically loaded distinction between the realm of religion and the realm of non-religion or the secular." My point here is neither to critique nor to defend the claims that Fitzgerald is making—though I think that he does provide valuable insights on the conceptualization of religion in the modern West. Rather, the point is that his project—to transform religious studies in part by ridding it of pervasive theological presuppositions—is itself thoroughly normative and concerns more than the norms of inquiry itself. While the scholar must be "freed" from this "ideological construct," the stakes are not merely academic. Fitzgerald is not concerned only with the norms of the discipline. Rather, the conception of religion developed and perpetuated by theologians, religious studies scholars, and others has played an important role in the legitimization of "the modern ideology of individualism and capitalism."[13] Given Fitzgerald's rhetoric, then, at stake are practical consequences for billions of people. These are normative judgments, making extensive claims about what ought to be—and what ought not to be.

Finally, we make normative claims whenever we try to identify "what is really going on here." To describe an experience as delusional or as transcendent, for instance, is to make a claim about the nature of reality. And such claims are normative in the relevant sense: they concern value judgments about the people and/or objects being studied.[14] This point comes out in a fascinating manner in Edward Slingerland's treatment of reductionism. Slingerland pursues the implications of what he describes as the "'embodied' approach to the study of culture," which sees "the human mind and its products as part of the physical world...."[15] Against the social constructivists he

---

[13] Fitzgerald, *Ideology of Religious Studies*, 7–8.

[14] There is a question whether a certain conception of discourse as nothing more than a language game can abstain from making the kinds of normative claims that I have in mind here. While that might be possible, were we to limit academic discourse to language conceived in this way, we would have to exclude most of what currently happens in the academy—particularly in the natural and social sciences—from the university.

[15] Edward Slingerland, "Who's Afraid of Reductionism? The Study of Religion in the Age of Cognitive Science," *Journal of the American Academy of Religion* 76, no. 2 (2008): 378.

criticizes, he holds that "this body-brain is no more than a very complex physical thing, a product of millions of years of evolution. Human thought is not a ghostly, disembodied process, but rather a series of body-brain states—a series of physical configurations of matter—each causing the next in accordance with the deterministic laws that govern the interactions of physical objects." At some level, we should adopt a physicalist perspective, not just as scholars, but as human beings: "Physicalism matters because it simply works better than dualism, and—once the reality of this superiority is fully grasped—this is an irresistibly powerful argument for creatures like us."[16] The tremendous achievements of modern medicine, based in this kind of physicalism, demonstrate this point.

Yet Slingerland's position is more interesting precisely because it argues against one set of normative implications that the "hard-core physicalists" (Slingerland's term for scholars such as Daniel Dennett) have claimed to find in this physicalism. Where they take this physicalism to entail that we should abandon all beliefs that depend on notions such as free will, Slingerland attempts to draw on a physicalist argument to avoid that particular normative claim. He views human beings as having been genetically "designed" to hold on to precisely the kinds of beliefs that hard-core physicalists want us to abandon. Thus, the hard-core physicalists are trying to fight precisely the kinds of biological mechanisms that they generally want to champion. Instead, Slingerland proposes living with a "dual consciousness, cultivating the ability to view human beings simultaneously under two descriptions: as physical systems and as persons."[17] Slingerland thereby claims that humans are right to hold on to—at one level— the beliefs that involve free will and to act accordingly. Admittedly, we might well ask whether Slingerland has given us any reason to think that we *should* cultivate a dual consciousness rather than face the perhaps Sisyphean task of trying to live without the "illusions" of viewing other human beings as persons and thinking we have a free will (as Slingerland's Dennett enjoins us) or whether the question is even coherent once one accepts an entirely deterministic view. (Slingerland's references to Kant, for instance, suggest that he has not grasped the challenge Kant poses to efforts to ground normativity

---

[16] Slingerland, "Who's Afraid of Reductionism?," 382–3, 402.
[17] Slingerland, "Who's Afraid of Reductionism?," 394, 402.

in the way that Slingerland implicitly does.[18]) My point here, however, is that Slingerland makes these normative claims—particularly, that we are right to adopt this dual consciousness.

Perhaps more importantly, in his discussion of hard-core physicalists he highlights the normative entailments of undermining someone's reasons for acting in a certain manner. Typically, if a belief in a transcendent being or a particular moral code can be shown to be caused by factors that the agent herself cannot recognize as constituting a good reason (such as a genetically based illusion), she should give up the belief. Insofar as I show someone's reasons for action to be based on a falsehood, I have thereby argued that she has no reason to act in that way—unless some other justification is given. Slingerland then takes it upon himself to provide this other justification, one grounded in physicalism itself. But the broader point is that much work in religious studies is normative precisely in undermining people's reasons for acting as they do. In doing so, it enjoins them—whether implicitly or explicitly—not to act in this way unless an alternative justification can be found.

The latter kinds of normativity highlight that we are not only making normative claims when we declare, "This is good," "This is orthodox," or "This is an abomination." The work of Nussbaum, Orsi, Fitzgerald, and Slingerland, for instance, is no less normative than the work of many theologians whose work might be considered suspect or inappropriate in religious studies. They offer examples of normative claims that seem clearly to belong within secular academia; but they are not relevantly different from the work of a "theologian" analyzing and defending—with extensive, reasoned arguments—Augustine's account of original sin as a distinctly Christian formulation of a universal human condition of finitude and a response of pride. Like those of this particular Augustinian theologian, the various claims described above presuppose (and sometimes make explicit) strong claims about the nature of human existence—and/or reality more generally—and have important consequences for how we should live. I focus on these kinds of claims, because they strike me

---

[18]   See, for instance, Slingerland, "Who's Afraid of Reductionism?," 385 and 402–3. My thinking on these matters in Kant is greatly indebted to conversations with Wesley Erdelack. Dan Arnold's critique of much work in cognitive science of religion is also directly relevant here; see my Chapter 1, above.

as precisely the type that are often given as grounds for excluding theology from the academic study of religion. Too often, we distinguish those who are explicitly doing normative work—ethicists, theologians, and philosophers of religion, for instance—from those who are doing more descriptive work—such as many historians—as engaged in fundamentally different activities. Instead of viewing this distinction as the difference that makes a difference for belonging in the field, I believe we should read it as shorthand for a different kind of distinction: all are making normative judgments; much of what distinguishes them is that the first category are *more likely* to be reflecting explicitly on the justification for their normative claims, whereas the second are more likely to focus their energy elsewhere. Insofar as the first group focus on the justification of the normative claims and the second group draw on normative claims to make further descriptive and explanatory claims, their predominant purposes may be distinguished. Nonetheless, both are making normative claims. Moreover, the movement between these different kinds of claims, by individual scholars as well as subfields, is far more frequent than we often acknowledge.

PRESUPPOSING RELIGION AS REASON'S OTHER

Be that as it may, however, the fact remains that many are much more comfortable with Nussbaum and Slingerland in the secular academy than with the Augustinian I just described. This contrast should provoke us to ask: Why do explicitly religious thinkers making normative claims raise so much more suspicion about their place in the modern, pluralistic university than a philosopher such as Nussbaum? This question returns us to the second of the presuppositions I identified above: that normative claims regarding religion are fundamentally matters of "faith" and not subject to reasoned argument. Much of the reason normative claims that are explicitly "religious" raise this suspicion while others do not is that much of our academic as well as other public discourse is shaped by a conception of religion as reason's other. Many of our discussions take for granted that religion is not something about which one can argue rationally. It is fundamentally about a "faith" that one either has or does not. This view finds powerful expression in the opening pages of Rudolf Otto's

The Idea of the Holy.[19] With everything resting on that, all subsequent argument is futile and/or trivial. Without a doubt, religion has often functioned in this way, and this arational strand has a long history in Christianity. But this conception received a significant boost in the wake of Enlightenment challenges to religion. Facing these challenges, one of the most prominent Protestant responses was a division of territory—a kind of non-competition agreement.[20] Religion would dominate—but be confined to—a realm that reason could not reach. Schleiermacher is a crucial figure in this tradition, though it seems to flow more from an oversimplification of his views than from his own vision. This tradition arguably lies behind much of the discourse on religion as *sui generis*, yet it is not limited to followers of Otto and Eliade.[21] William James's *Varieties of Religious Experience*, for instance, easily has a similar effect: directing our attention to a "branch" of religion occupying a sphere that reason cannot reach.[22]

Though few would defend this conception of religion in the simple form I have sketched it here, it nonetheless seems to have a surprising degree of influence—at least in the United States. It is used to justify excluding "religion" as a whole from the university as well as to defend religious claims from rational criticism. It is the hidden, shared presupposition in many disagreements between religion's critics and its defenders. I suspect it also operates in the work of a number of contemporary continental philosophers whose call for a return to religion appears motivated in part by their views on the limits of reason. If reason fails, turn elsewhere—i.e., to religion. And it is both powerful and dangerous in our public political discussions: It frequently leads us to presuppose that meaningful, reasoned debate

---

[19] Rudolf Otto, *The Idea of the Holy: An Inquiry into the Non-Rational Factor in the Idea of the Divine and Its Relation to the Rational*, trans. John W. Harvey, 2nd edn. (Oxford: Oxford University Press, 1958), 1–11. See my further discussion of Otto below.

[20] For an extended treatment of a competing Protestant response, see my *Religion, Modernity, and Politics in Hegel* (Oxford: Oxford University Press, 2011).

[21] For an excellent discussion of related matters in terms of the "sacred/profane" dichotomy, see Robert A. Orsi, "Everyday Miracles: The Study of Lived Religion," in *Lived Religion in America: Toward a History of Practice*, ed. David D. Hall (Princeton: Princeton University Press, 1997), 3–21, especially 5–7.

[22] William James, *The Varieties of Religious Experience* (Cambridge: Harvard University Press, 1985). Of course, there are serious questions regarding the adequacy of that interpretation of James's project. I am grateful to Matthew Bagger for discussions on this point.

on topics such as reproductive freedom or gay rights is impossible and consequently not worth attempting. On both sides, positions are further polarized by an unwillingness to search for common ground that would enable reasoned exchange. For some, appeals to "faith" function as a trump card that purportedly excuses them from the need to provide arguments. As noted above, this is one of the most significant ways in which discussions of religion continue to be shaped by an unacknowledged but specific theological vision, even if this view is far less representative of Protestantism as a whole than many contend.

In arguing that this conception of religion should not be foundational to the discipline, it is important to demonstrate the ways in which this conception is inadequate. The focus on norms and their justification illustrates this inadequacy well. If we frame the discussion in terms of normativity, the crucial issue becomes whether someone is willing to offer an argument or justification for a norm—and, accordingly, what counts as offering an argument. There can and should be much debate about what counts as "giving an argument" in the context of the academic study of religion. I want to suggest that in thinking about the discipline as a whole we should conceive of this process broadly enough to encompass a wide range of justificatory strategies. For instance, arguments need not conform to a foundationalist epistemological model—a view in which, in order to be justified, a belief must be shown to be derivable from foundations that are not themselves derived or inferred from other claims. Conceiving of the possibilities broadly does not mean one has to agree with them all, but we should not necessarily exclude people from the field just because we do not agree with the arguments they offer in favor of their positions. Broadly speaking, then, I propose that we navigate between the Scylla of an overly stringent demand for arguments conforming to a very narrow model (that would exclude pragmatism, for instance) and the Charybdis of the notion that all views ultimately depend upon equally arbitrary and indefensible presuppositions.

As we seek to illuminate what it can mean to offer an argument for a position, it is vital to emphasize the breadth of possibilities. One set of strategies includes various forms of foundationalism, arguments that seek to trace the justifications for any given claim back to a non-inferential claim that is considered basic. Though different, appeals to purportedly universal human experiences—of the sort that Nussbaum argues for—also enter the realm of debate. We can argue, for all kinds of reasons, against the universality of these experiences, and it is this space for argument that is essential.

In the neo-pragmatist tradition, Jeffrey Stout has sought to bring our attention to the diversity of argumentative strategies that we use in our everyday discourse on public matters, including religion, in pluralistic societies. Rejecting the idea that once we come to the topic of religion, all argument stops—i.e., that religion is a conversation-stopper—Stout stresses the important role of immanent criticism, in which we start with the other person's own viewpoint and argue that in some respect it contradicts itself and/or should lead to another conclusion than the person thinks.[23] Championing the pervasiveness and power of immanent criticism over against John Rawls's conception of public reason, Stout writes:

> Immanent criticism is both one of the most widely used forms of reasoning in what I would call public political discourse and one of the most effective ways of showing respect for fellow citizens who hold differing points of view. Any speaker is free to request reasons from any other. If I have access to the right forum, I can tell the entire community what reasons move me to accept a given conclusion, thus showing my fellow citizens respect as requesters of my reasons. But to explain to them why *they* might have reason to agree with me, given their different collateral premises, I might well have to proceed piecemeal, addressing one individual (or one type of perspective) at a time.[24]

The non-confessional university is a public forum in just this sense, and immanent criticism will be one important way in which we argue with others in this context. Perhaps more importantly, it is a context in which "[a]ny speaker is free to request reasons from any other." That sentence expresses well a basic feature of this setting: no claim is beyond questioning.

In a different intellectual lineage, despite the challenges he seeks to pose to the modern academy through his championing of tradition, Alasdair MacIntyre offers another model of providing argument in

---

[23] Stout's work is particularly relevant because one of his significant targets is the claim—made but subsequently disavowed by another neo-pragmatist, Richard Rorty—that religion is a conversation stopper. See Richard Rorty, "Religion as a Conversation-stopper," in *Philosophy and Social Hope* (London: Penguin Books, 1999), 168–74. Rorty has revised his position in "Religion in the Public Square: A Reconsideration," *Journal of Religious Ethics* 31, no. 1 (2003): 141–9.

[24] Jeffrey Stout, *Democracy and Tradition* (Princeton: Princeton University Press, 2004), 73.

support of a position. Rejecting what he sees as the Enlightenment ideal of arguments standing free of tradition and appealing to a universal audience, MacIntyre articulates and defends a model of reason as necessarily borne by—rather than an alternative to—tradition. His argument that traditions are frequently incommensurable poses grave challenges to rational dialogue among those who do not share a tradition.[25] Though such reasoned exchange between those not sharing a tradition is possible, it requires learning the other tradition as a "second first language" and then providing an account of the other tradition as a whole. Providing a rational argument to the other person will often require demonstrating that one's own tradition can explain the other tradition—its successes as well as its failures—more effectively than it can explain itself.[26] While argument across traditions is possible, then, it requires a level of engagement that will be rare; for the most part, the best we can do is to face the world from within a coherent tradition, relinquishing the universalistic hope of providing arguments that can appeal to everyone.

The folly of the modern university is closely tied to its failure to recognize this difficulty. MacIntyre takes the modern secular academy to be largely based upon an ultimately indefensible conception of reason as standing independent of traditions of inquiry.[27] And yet, over the course of several books and many articles, he develops a complex and widely influential argument for his position.[28] He seeks to undermine the coherence of alternative conceptions of reason and to demonstrate that to appeal to tradition in the manner that he does is not irrational. He demonstrates that latter point at greatest length in *Whose Justice? Which Rationality?*, where he argues that we must understand a tradition at any given point in time in terms of the dilemmas and perplexities whose resolution gave rise to it. Reflecting the power of MacIntyre's arguments to appeal to and persuade many

[25] Alasdair C. MacIntyre, *Whose Justice? Which Rationality?* (Notre Dame, IN: University of Notre Dame Press, 1988), chapter 19. I have treated MacIntyre on these issues at greater length in Thomas A. Lewis, "On the Limits of Narrative: Communities in Pluralistic Society," *Journal of Religion* 86, no. 1 (2006): 55–80.

[26] Alasdair C. MacIntyre, *Three Rival Versions of Moral Enquiry: Encyclopedia, Genealogy, and Tradition* (Notre Dame, IN: University of Notre Dame Press, 1990), 117–21.

[27] MacIntyre, *Three Rival Versions*, especially 216–36.

[28] See, in particular, Alasdair C. MacIntyre, *After Virtue: A Study in Moral Theory*, 2nd edn. (Notre Dame, IN: University of Notre Dame Press, 1984); *Whose Justice? Which Rationality?*; and *Three Rival Versions*.

people who did not previously share a tradition with him, MacIntyre's thought has won great attention and acclaim in precisely the academic context that he holds generally lacks the practices necessary to support the model of inquiry that he defends. Despite MacIntyre's stated rejection of the Enlightenment goal of appealing to a universal audience, then, it would be misleading to suggest that MacIntyre is unwilling to offer arguments to defend the normative claims he makes—arguments that appeal to more than a limited community that already shares his presuppositions.[29]

Discussing these examples so briefly, some may appear unconvincing. One might contend, for instance, that MacIntyre has abandoned—in theory and practice—the goal of making an argument that appeals to more than a limited community sharing a set of practices that are not shared by the modern academy as a whole. There is certainly room for argument. But that is the point: there is room for argument. And the arguments can be made without appealing to transcendent authority and without presupposing "faith."

To say that a scholar must be willing to provide reasons for any particular claim or position, however, does not entail that she must do so in every piece of writing or even that every scholar must count doing so as within her areas of specialization. Just as an economist might make use of game theory without providing an extensive justification of its validity, so scholars of religion may produce works that take certain claims for granted within that context. Doing so only becomes problematic when the scholar declares those presuppositions to be illegitimate objects of inquiry. Part of the academic enterprise is that, when pressed, a scholar should admit the importance of being able to offer such a defense. We do not need to write a philosophical treatise every time we use the word "cruel," but we need to be willing to accept the concept of "cruelty" as a legitimate issue for inquiry. (It is likely the case that scholars of religion encounter claims that a particular authority or experience is beyond question more frequently than scholars in many other disciplines, but I suspect that the same dynamic is common to other fields as well.)

---

[29] Building on this point, we might argue that Hegel ultimately offers a better account of the strongest elements of MacIntyre's project than MacIntyre himself does. Drawing out the Hegelian background also suggests the connections to Stout's pragmatism, in which Hegel also serves as a crucial source. On Hegel and MacIntyre, see my *Religion, Modernity, and Politics in Hegel*, 187–202.

In defining broadly what it means to offer justification for our normative claims, I seek to define religious studies inclusively. I would err on the side of inclusiveness with regard to the kinds of arguments that might be offered. We might not agree with the arguments, but as we try to conceive of the field as a whole, we should be slow to rule arguments simply out of bounds.

Yet even if this broad conception of offering an argument provides us with a generally irenic conception, there is also a rub. The vision of the study of religion that I am proposing does require everyone to be willing to debate—and in doing so to submit to critique and criticism— their normative claims. No claim or canon can stand as unquestionable or as free of the need for justification of its authoritative status. To cordon off a set of texts, a body of doctrines, or a church office holder as simply "givens," whose normative status requires no justification or cannot be argued about, is to remove oneself from this discussion. Thus, another Augustinian theologian—different from the one above—who incorporates in his analysis of Augustine claims about the unquestionable authority of Augustine as a Church Father or of the New Testament texts on which Augustine draws places himself beyond the bounds of the academic study of religion.

Perhaps more significantly in the present context, appeals to anything like private revelation or unique experiences do not allow much basis for conversation if this is the only justification someone is willing to offer. Take the opening of the third chapter of Rudolf Otto's *Idea of the Holy*:

> The reader is invited to direct his mind to a moment of deeply-felt religious experience, as little as possible qualified by other forms of consciousness. Whoever cannot do this, whoever knows no such moments in his experience, is requested to read no further; for it is not easy to discuss questions of religious psychology with one who can recollect the emotions of his adolescence, the discomforts of indigestion, or, say, social feelings, but cannot recall any intrinsically religious feelings.[30]

Otto does far more here than refer to individual experience; he informs the reader that if she is incapable of relating to this experience, he is no longer interested in engaging with her. When an author makes this rhetorical move, he or she removes him- or herself from a

---

[30] Otto, *The Idea of the Holy*, 8.

discussion in which claims are arbitrated through argument, for to make this move is to step out of the practice of giving and asking for reasons and to appeal to the purported givenness of an individual experience. "I had a feeling..." is, in itself, no more relevant as evidence in the study of religion than in the study of literature or economics. If we have not had this experience, then Otto—at least in this passage—claims to have nothing to say to us: he has no argument to offer.[31]

Of course, many believers from many religions make these kinds of moves. I am not claiming that they should not. But in making claims of this sort, individuals remove themselves from the realm of academic discourse. They are not basing their claims on grounds that are in any sense subject to constructive debate by a larger community.

Focusing on normativity and the arguments brought to defend normative claims shifts the debate over the work appropriate to the academic study of religion from the theology-v.-religious-studies standstill—which too often leaves us wondering exactly how far the debate has come since the 1960s and 1970s—to more promising ground. And because debates about the nature of reason and argument are by no means unique to the study of religion, doing so also demonstrates that the substantive issues genuinely at stake here in the study of religion are the same as those in many other departments around the university. In showing that our problems are not unique but are rather the same as those in many other fields, this shift can help us to better articulate the ways in which we do belong in the non-confessional university.

At the same time, it leaves space for diverse approaches within religious studies. Too often our discussions of what is proper in the study of religion sound as if there should be one way of doing religious studies. Against such presuppositions, I think the strength of the discipline derives in large part from the plurality of types of investigations we conduct and questions we ask.

Finally, with an eye toward broader issues, let me close with what is perhaps the most practically significant—not "merely academic"—reason for reframing the debate in this manner. The simple juxtaposing of theology and religious studies is too often premised on an assumption that religion is fundamentally non-rational. Whether

---

[31] Whether Otto qualifies this point elsewhere in his work I leave as an open question. My point concerns this rhetorical move rather than an overall reading of Otto.

understood as an irrational superstition, as based in feeling and intuition, and/or as an irreducibly personal experience, religion understood in this manner becomes something about which reasoned exchange is impossible. In accepting this picture and portraying theology as antithetical to reasoned inquiry, adamant secularists unwittingly join forces with anti-intellectual adherents of religious traditions in supporting the idea that we cannot engage religious ideas constructively. One of the greatest costs of allocating religion such a small role in public and secular education in the United States is that it results in broad swaths of the population—including many educated elites—who never question that faith is some primordial given about which it is impossible to reason. The public discourse about religion that results is remarkably uninformed and uncritical. Ultimately, then, one of the most important reasons for recasting the theoretical issues at stake in defining the academic study of religion in the university is that it educates people to think more critically about religious claims.

3

History in the Future of the Philosophy of Religion

As reason goes, so goes the philosophy of religion. So might we organize much recent work in philosophy of religion. We can usefully think in terms of three broad camps: (1) those who would develop the philosophy of religion on the basis of generally universalistic conceptions of reason; (2) those who adopt one of a variety of historicist conceptions of reason; and (3) those who adopt more radical critiques of reason, sometimes turning to religion as an alternative to what they see as a failing reason. Those in the first camp aspire to give reasons that can appeal to all mature subjects everywhere. In this vision, one does not need a particular background, a common experience, or a shared historical context in order to appreciate reasons—as long as they are genuine reasons. The second group is perhaps the most varied: I have in mind a range of views in which what counts as a reason is context dependent, where the context is typically defined in terms of social and historical processes. I refer to these collectively as views of the historicity of reason. Hegel can be seen as offering one version; pragmatists offer others; Reformed Epistemology offers yet others. Where the second group rejects universalistic conceptions of reason in favor of more historically embedded ones, the third views the second as being satisfied with half measures in its critique of Enlightenment conceptions of reason. Drawing not only on Nietzsche but also on more postmodern or poststructuralist theories, they frequently turn from philosophy to religion, as in Hent de Vries's *Philosophy and the Turn to Religion*.[1]

---

[1] Hent de Vries, *Philosophy and the Turn to Religion* (Baltimore: Johns Hopkins University Press, 1999). For another influential example, see Alain Badiou, *Saint Paul:*

While a great deal of work continues to be done in the first and third groups, the second group—which might be conceived as seeking a middle path between the other two—is arguably generating some of the most important work of late. We see this in the central position of Reformed Epistemology in analytic philosophy of religion as well as in the prominence of pragmatism in a great deal of work in philosophy of religion and religious ethics.[2] In terms of particular figures, we see it in the impact of Alasdair MacIntyre, Jeffrey Stout, Charles Taylor, and Nicholas Wolterstorff in these and other subfields. For many who have been shaped by this family of accounts of reason, historicist conceptions of reason have supported a turn to history: careful attention to historical figures in order to understand better the sources and contexts of our own thinking and reasoning. In some cases, turning to history has entailed more than turning to historical figures; it has also included carefully situating these figures in their social and political contexts. While I take both aspects of this shift to be important—as demonstrated in the discussion of Amy Hollywood's work in Chapter 1—I am most concerned in this chapter with the more basic point of the significance of turning to these earlier figures.

Charles Taylor, Richard Rorty, and Jennifer Herdt have developed powerful arguments that this kind of historical inquiry is normatively significant.[3] It is no mere accessory to explicitly normative and

---

The Foundations of Universalism, trans. Ray Brassier (Stanford: Stanford University Press, 2003).

[2] On Reformed Epistemology and its impact, see Chapter 1. For important pragmatist interventions, see Nancy K. Frankenberry, ed., *Radical Interpretation in Religion* (Cambridge: Cambridge University Press, 2002); G. Scott Davis, *Believing and Acting: The Pragmatic Turn in Comparative Religion and Ethics* (Oxford: Oxford University Press, 2012); Jeffrey Stout, *Ethics after Babel: The Languages of Morals and Their Discontents*, 1st Princeton edn. (Princeton: Princeton University Press, 2001); and Jeffrey Stout, *Democracy and Tradition* (Princeton: Princeton University Press, 2004).

[3] See, in particular, Charles Taylor, "Philosophy and Its History," in *Philosophy in History: Essays in the Historiography of Philosophy*, ed. Richard Rorty, J. B Schneewind, and Quentin Skinner (Cambridge: Cambridge University Press, 1984), 17–30; Charles Taylor, "Comparison, History, Truth," in *Myth and Philosophy*, ed. Frank Reynolds and David Tracy (Albany: State University of New York Press, 1990), 37–55; Richard Rorty, "The Historiography of Philosophy: Four Genres," in Rorty, Schneewind, and Skinner, *Philosophy in History*, 49–75; and Jennifer A. Herdt, "Religious Ethics, History, and the Rise of Modern Moral Philosophy: Focus Introduction," *Journal of Religious Ethics* 28, no. 2 (2000): 165–88.

constructive work but rather integral thereto. Of course, one need not accept a historicist conception of reason to think it worthwhile to turn to the history of ideas, yet historicist conceptions of reason give us additional reasons for turning to history as we seek to understand our contemporary options. Amidst this family of approaches, the justifications for and corresponding fruits of turning to history are multiple. Perhaps most obviously, if we hold that what counts as a reason and what counts as a significant question for any given audience are crucially shaped by history, then interrogating our history will be vital to seeing how we have come to frame problems as we do. It is incumbent upon us to understand how we arrived where we are—to trace the way that major questions in the philosophy of religion have developed and transformed over time. Such investigations construct narratives of our own genesis, with the insight that grasping how our present commitments have been formed will play an essential role in grasping the respects in which they are justified and the respects in which they require revision.[4] Beyond illuminating the path we have taken to arrive where we are, investigating our history may also disclose paths not taken. We may discover alternatives that we then seek to champion as superior to the path actually taken—as a better way of framing the questions and/or answering them. In other cases, we may examine a view that was an option at one point in our history but that—due to subsequent developments that we cannot undo—is no longer an option for us. A particular way of thinking of oneself, for instance, may have been inextricable from social relations—such as those of European feudalism—that are no longer extant today. In this mode, then, the investigation of history serves to expose whom we could have been or perhaps still can be. In some versions of this second mode, historical studies may uncover alternatives that were not simply not taken but were marginalized, occluded, or blocked by the developments that dominated. Historical inquiry here exposes the underside of the developments that are in the fore in an account such as Taylor's. While this conception of historical study is often associated with Marxist and Nietzschean approaches, there is no reason to think that attending to the underside of specific

---

[4] Charles Taylor's *Sources of the Self: The Making of the Modern Identity* (Cambridge: Harvard University Press, 1989) remains a paradigmatic example of this model of turning to history in order to understand whom we have become.

dominant developments commits one to a Marxist, Nietzschean, or Foucaultian genealogical vision.[5]

Rather than developing these rationales, this chapter focuses on a more specific aspect of the role of history in philosophy of religion's future.[6] I seek to bring this turn to history in philosophy of religion together with another such turn.

While important work in philosophy of religion has been interrogating its past, other subfields of religious studies have been engaged in another turn to history. Much recent work has focused on the history of the study of religion. Although many works have contributed to this development, some of the most prominent and widely discussed are Tomoko Masuzawa's *The Invention of World Religions*, Hans Kippenberg's *Discovering Religious History in the Modern Age*, David Chidester's *Savage Systems*, and Jonathan Z. Smith's influential chapter, "Religion, Religions, Religious."[7] Across their differences, these works attend to and illuminate the history of religion's construction as a topic. Where one might be tempted to treat histories of the field as instances of academic navel gazing, this body of work has argued convincingly that this history is interwoven with the term's use in a variety of political, economic, administrative, and other public contexts and thereby implicated in the global dominance of particular people and agendas. Defining religion has been far more than a "merely academic" exercise. In revealing the political stakes and implications of the history of religion's conceptualization, these currents in the field have demonstrated the importance of interrogating this history.

---

[5] A fourth noteworthy function of such studies of history can be to authorize the scholar's own view. Situating oneself in an authoritative tradition may function largely to legitimate one's position. This strategy is particularly significant in the context of religious traditions in which "the tradition" itself is recognized as in some sense authoritative.

[6] I return in the Conclusion to the conceptualization of turning to history.

[7] Tomoko Masuzawa, *The Invention of World Religions, Or, How European Universalism Was Preserved in the Language of Pluralism* (Chicago: University of Chicago Press, 2005); Hans G. Kippenberg, *Discovering Religious History in the Modern Age*, trans. Barbara Harshav (Princeton: Princeton University Press, 2002); David Chidester, *Savage Systems: Colonialism and Comparative Religion in Southern Africa* (Charlottesville: University Press of Virginia, 1996); and Jonathan Z. Smith, "Religion, Religions, Religious," in *Critical Terms for Religious Studies*, ed. Mark C. Taylor (Chicago: University of Chicago Press, 1998), 269–84.

This chapter seeks to bring together these two turns to history—to that of philosophy of religion and to that of the conceptualization of religion—in order to show the way they should inform each other and in important respects overlap. Doing so reveals how the study of philosophy of religion's history can be informed by broader concerns about the history of the study of religion as well as what the history of philosophy of religion can contribute to these broader histories of the conceptualization of religion. It shows how two sets of conversations—which to date have often taken place separately—can and should be brought together to mutually enrich each other. The contributions go in both directions, but bringing these conversations together particularly shows the potential of philosophy of religion to contribute to broader discussions in the field—especially when the former is informed by the latter. More concretely, conceiving of the projects of influential figures in the modern history of philosophy of religion as attempting to transform the contested category of religion itself illuminates the centrality of philosophy of religion to religious studies as a whole.

To develop and illustrate this point, I offer two brief case studies from what is often seen as a founding moment in modern Western philosophy of religion: the late-eighteenth and early nineteenth-century German context. While many moments are worth exploring, this period is simultaneously especially potent for the history of philosophy of religion and—relatedly—one of the key sites of the emergence of the modern academic study of religion.[8] Although scholars such as Kippenberg and Masuzawa have generally attended more to the emerging social sciences and philology than to the philosophy of religion, they demonstrate how dramatically European conceptions of religion were transforming during this period. The category itself was highly contested—as a result of Enlightenment critiques, the development of natural sciences, social upheavals, the ongoing working out of the Protestant Reformation, and encounters with other cultures as a result of European trade and colonialism. Attending to the development of philosophy of religion during this period—partially pursued in the kinds of historical studies mentioned

---

[8]   See, for instance, David Tracy, "On the Origins of the Philosophy of Religion: The Need for a New Narrative of Its Founding," in Reynolds and Tracy, *Myth and Philosophy*, 11–36, which focuses on Hume, Kant, and Hegel. Kippenberg's *Discovering Religious History in the Modern Age* also begins here.

above but, to date, with inadequate attention to the philosophy—will do much to illuminate this history's importance for the broader field of religious studies.

It is not hard to see figures such as Kant, Schleiermacher, and Hegel as trying to make sense of the religious traditions they inherited in light of the many challenges that had been posed by the Enlightenment and its aftermath. But their works are just as much attempts to redefine the category of religion itself at a moment when it had been profoundly destabilized. I focus here on what can be gained by framing their contributions in terms of the reconceptualization of this contested term.

Specifically, I consider two of the most influential figures of this period, Friedrich Schleiermacher (1768–1834) and G. W. F. Hegel (1770–1831). While both are canonical figures who have been influential across numerous disciplines, I concentrate on their competing visions of the concept of religion itself. Each offers a powerful—and very different—defense of religion in the face of widespread intellectual and social challenges and upheavals; and in both cases the defense turns on the reconceptualization of the object, religion. Yet while both of these figures have already been voluminously analyzed, it is remarkable how little scholarship has focused directly on their conceptualizations of religion. To make the task more manageable within one chapter, the discussion will be limited to Schleiermacher's original, 1799 edition of *On Religion: Speeches to Its Cultured Despisers* and to Hegel's Berlin lectures on the philosophy of religion, particularly those from 1827.[9] Even a relatively brief treatment of these materials places in relief both their centrality to the history of the study of religion in the West and how much we gain by framing their contributions in terms of the reconceptualization of religion.

---

[9] Friedrich Schleiermacher, *On Religion: Speeches to Its Cultured Despisers*, trans. Richard Crouter (Cambridge: Cambridge University Press, 1996). In focusing on the 1799 edition, I leave aside important questions about the relation between the first edition and later ones as well as the relation between *On Religion* and *The Christian Faith*. For the latter, see Friedrich Schleiermacher, *The Christian Faith*, trans. James S. Stewart and H. R. Mackintosh (Edinburgh: T&T Clark, 1999). For Hegel, see G. W. F. Hegel, *Vorlesungen über die Philosophie der Religion*, ed. Walter Jaeschke, 3 vols. (Hamburg: Felix Meiner Verlag, 1983); G. W. F. Hegel, *Lectures on the Philosophy of Religion*, trans. R. F. Brown, P. C. Hodgson, and J. M. Stewart, 3 vols. (Berkeley: University of California Press, 1984). For ease of reference, I cite these by the pagination from the German edition, which is included in the margins of the English translation.

FRIEDRICH SCHLEIERMACHER'S RECONCEPTUALIZATION OF RELIGION'S ESSENCE

Writing to address the Berlin salon society in which he circulated, Schleiermacher directs *On Religion* to cultured elites who frequently look down on the religion of the masses as beneath them. The dynamics of the situation remain resonant today. The core of his approach to persuading his audience of religion's ongoing relevance lies in convincing them that their dismissals of religion are based on misconceiving the object. What they have taken to be religion is far from its essence. Grasping religion's essence will enable them to dismiss corrupted forms of religion as just that—attenuated or degenerate manifestations—while appreciating that religion at its core relates closely to the concerns of these cultural elites.

The second of the five speeches, "The Essence of Religion," is defined by the question, "What is religion?" Schleiermacher urges his audience to abjure their preconceptions and "stand before the holy circles with the most unprejudiced sobriety of mind . . . neither seduced by old memories nor corrupted by preconceived suspicions . . . ."[10] Appreciating what religion really is requires distinguishing it from what it has often been taken to be. Metaphysics and morality are contrasted with religion, so that "you must be honest enough to restore to both parts of philosophy what belongs to them and admit that you are still ignorant of what concerns religion."[11] Schleiermacher rehabilitates religion by conceptualizing it in a way that distinguishes it from both theoretical and practical philosophy:

> In order to take possession of its own domain, religion renounces herewith all claims to whatever belongs to those others and gives back everything that has been forced upon it. It does not wish to determine and explain the universe according to its nature as does metaphysics; it does not desire to continue the universe's development and perfect it by the power of freedom and the divine free choice of a human being as does morals. Religion's essence is neither thinking nor acting, but intuition and feeling. It wishes to intuit the universe.[12]

---

[10] Schleiermacher, *On Religion*, 18.   [11] Schleiermacher, *On Religion*, 21.

[12] Schleiermacher, *On Religion*, 22. While one might take this claim as grounds for designating Schleiermacher's project as outside the bounds of *philosophy* of religion, doing so would prematurely rule out far too much.

Religion is to be preserved by being properly distinguished from philosophy.

To focus on religion's essence, for Schleiermacher, is to focus on the intuition and corresponding feeling at religion's core. Religion begins with an "intuition of the universe."[13] To grasp religion, we must focus on this immediate experience, prior to and more fundamental than efforts to incorporate these experiences into systematic structures: "Intuition is and always remains something individual, set apart, the immediate perception, nothing more. To bind it and to incorporate it into a whole is once more the business not of sense but of abstract thought. The same is true of religion; it stops with the immediate experiences of the existence and action of the universe, with the individual intuitions and feelings...."[14] Religion's essence then, is found in our largely passive response to the universe's impingement upon us. As we move away from the immediacy of this originary experience, we corrupt or at least distort it.

The notions of intuition and feeling that Schleiermacher makes central to religion have been one of the principal nodes of dispute in debates over his work and legacy.[15] Schleiermacher's emphasis on the immediacy of religious experience has been widely taken to be a key point of origin for protective strategies—notions of religion that serve to isolate and thereby defend religion from a host of challenges. Wayne Proudfoot, for instance, has influentially argued that Schleiermacher's claims to the immediacy of religious intuition and feeling are simultaneously essential to his larger project and fatally flawed: "The religious consciousness is said to have the immediacy and independence from thought which are characteristic of sensations," which function to protect it from Kantian concerns about the conditioned character of the understanding, "and yet to include an intuitive component whose object is the infinite," thus giving it a significance lacking in ordinary sensations on their own.[16] Without concepts, Proudfoot argues, it is impossible to conceive the object of this intuition in terms of the universe, the whole, or the infinite. Without concepts, no determinate object is possible. Thus, Schleiermacher's

---

[13] Schleiermacher, *On Religion*, 24.   [14] Schleiermacher, *On Religion*, 26.

[15] Intuition would eventually drop out of later editions of the *Speeches*, leaving the last edition as well as *The Christian Faith* to focus on feeling rather than intuition and feeling.

[16] Wayne Proudfoot, *Religious Experience* (Berkeley: University of California Press, 1985), 11; see also 3–15.

attempt to maintain both the immediacy of the intuition *and* a particular object for it undermine the project. Despite this fatal flaw, Proudfoot argues, Schleiermacher's protective strategy of defending religion by seeking to preserve its autonomy has decisively molded modern philosophy of religion. Further developed in figures such as Rudolf Otto, Joachim Wach, and Mircea Eliade, this general strategy—according to Proudfoot—continues to profoundly shape philosophy of religion today.

Andrew Dole has raised important challenges to Proudfoot's reading of Schleiermacher's project as well as its legacy. With regard to his legacy, Dole has argued that Schleiermacher should not be seen as the crucial progenitor of Otto and Eliade. While they, particularly Otto, claim to find in Schleiermacher's *On Religion* key precedents of their work, their protectionist strategies stand in deep tension with Schleiermacher's own religious naturalism.[17] With regard to the notion of immediacy itself, Dole gives it strikingly little attention. Nonetheless, he argues there are few textual grounds for claiming that Schleiermacher views religious experience as "self-authenticating" and rejects such interpretations.[18] Moreover, drawing on the work of Trutz Rendtorff, Dole develops a deeply social reading of Schleiermacher's *On Religion*. Religion is thus not grounded in an immediate, private experience. While Dole does not focus on the concept of immediacy, the implication seems to be that Schleiermacher's claims about immediacy must be subordinated to his claims about sociality and interpreted accordingly. In this respect, Dole effectively contends that Schleiermacher's account of religion's essence is best interpreted not simply in relation to Kantian worries about the conditioned character of experience and knowledge (central to Proudfoot's interpretation) but also in relation to a turn toward intersubjectivity that is more prominent in Hegel's thought.[19] While I find much that is compelling in Dole's interpretation, without attending more extensively to Schleiermacher's explicit claims about immediacy, as well as passivity, it is difficult to judge whether Dole's interpretive strategy can fully account for those sections of the text.

[17] See Andrew Dole, "Schleiermacher and Otto on Religion," *Religious Studies* 40, no. 4 (2004): 389–413, and Andrew Dole, *Schleiermacher on Religion and the Natural Order* (Oxford: Oxford University Press, 2010).

[18] Dole, *Schleiermacher on Religion*, 168–70. On the relation to the notion of immediacy, see 234 n. 59.

[19] Dole, *Schleiermacher on Religion*, 22–3, 84–7, and 105–14.

Fortunately, we need not resolve these interpretive debates in order to recognize the stakes of the history of religion's conceptualization. To the contrary, precisely in the debate over immediacy we can see how implicated this history is in ongoing discussions. Our understanding of Schleiermacher and the effects of his thought on nineteenth- and twentieth-century conceptions of religion bears directly on our understanding of the study of religion today—both how it came to be shaped as it is as well as what its current prospects are. For this reason, we cannot be satisfied with broad brush accounts of figures such as Schleiermacher; we need the kind of subtle analysis of their philosophical claims that philosophers of religion can bring.

In the remainder of *On Religion*, Schleiermacher nuances his claims about religion's essence in a manner that connects his account of religion's essence to many other phenomena conventionally referred to as religion. As Dole convincingly argues, religion—for Schleiermacher—comprises more than its essence.[20] While the focus on intuition and feeling discussed above dominates Schleiermacher's second speech, the following speeches demonstrate the way that Schleiermacher uses this notion as a criterion for determining ways in which much else—associations, institutions, doctrines, and behavioral codes—may be appropriate and legitimate developments *or* attenuated, corrupted manifestations of this essence. Schleiermacher spends some time sketching an account of ideal expressions of the impulse to communicate religious intuitions and to form communities in which to share them, but he devotes greater attention to setting out the connection he sees between religion's essence and the actual forms that religion takes.[21] His account of religion's essence, then, does not radically separate this essence from everything else that may be called religious. In discussing the plurality of positive religions, Schleiermacher maintains his highly critical tone toward most existing religious institutions yet insists that even here one can—and should—penetrate the corrupted form to identify the vital intuition at the root of the religion:

> [H]owever deep this corruption may be rooted in these religions, and however much they may have suffered under this, yet consider also that

---

[20] Dole, *Schleiermacher on Religion*, 72–90.
[21] On the first point, see, for instance, Schleiermacher, *On Religion*, 88–9. On the second, see 73 and 100.

it is the properly religious view of all things to seek every trace of the divine, the true, and the eternal, even in what appears to us to be vulgar and base, and to worship even the most distant trace.... [Y]ou will still find more than distant traces of divinity.[22]

Precisely those manifestations that Schleiermacher derides are here conceived as degenerate and attenuated forms of religion's essence. They merit examining as religion, even if they deserve strident criticism as well. The examination of these corrupted forms, for Schleiermacher, should consist in uncovering the intuition of the universe that gave impetus to the particular religion: instead of "shrink[ing] back in fright" at the messy and disappointing actualities of particular religions, "dig even deeper where your magic rod has once struck, and you will certainly unearth the heavenly."[23] At the religion's foundation lies its particular intuition of the universe.

This degeneration results from the attenuation of the connection to the original experience and/or the corruption of these forms by external influences, such as the pettiness fostered by bourgeois life and the intrusion of political interests. While such corruption is pervasive and to some degree historically inevitable, it is not intrinsic to the concept of religion. It lies neither in religion's essence nor in the appropriate and legitimate impulse to communicate this intuition in communities and to allow it to inform one's life as a whole. In the defense of Christianity's superiority in the fifth speech, he contends that "Christianity has thus made first and essential the demand that religiousness shall be a continuum in human life, and it scorns being satisfied with the strongest expression of religiousness as soon as it is supposed to pertain to and govern only certain parts of life."[24] Schleiermacher is vague about the nature of this informing of all parts of life: his earlier discussions of religion and politics entail that he cannot be calling for a political system shaped by Christian doctrinal claims; yet passages such as this reject the notion that religion should have no bearing whatsoever on realms such as ethics and politics.

The notion of religion's essence, then, functions not as a boundary circumscribing the entirety of religion but as a principle by which to interpret religion and to determine whether other instances of religion are legitimate, authentic expressions of this essence or are distortions

---

[22] Schleiermacher, *On Religion*, 99; see also 96 and 111.
[23] Schleiermacher, *On Religion*, 111.   [24] Schleiermacher, *On Religion*, 118.

thereof.[25] While the point might seem trivial, it is an important correction to readings of Schleiermacher—as well as of Schleiermacher as a stand-in for a reified "Protestant conception of religion"—that take religion as a whole to be comprised exclusively by the intuitions and feelings so central to his discussion in the second speech. That which bothered the "cultured despisers" in his audience as well as many today—whether understood as cumbersome orthodoxies, ossified rituals, or inappropriate involvement in politics—are part of religion, even if they are a corrupted form. They are neither accepted as legitimate forms of religion nor simply dismissed as not being religion at all.

Given our present concern with the conceptualization of religion, what matters most here is not the precise criterion for distinguishing ideal from actual religion but the notion that religion's authentic forms flow from this immediate intuition of the universe. Its actual forms most often suffer from an ossified relation to the original intuitions that founded the tradition as well as their contamination by external interests. On one hand, Schleiermacher's conception of religion does not separate religion as radically from everything else—such as daily life and politics—as is often claimed. On the other hand, praiseworthy and degenerate forms of religion are distinguished according to the way that they are related to the underlying intuition of the universe. Thus, even though more nuanced than the images (or caricatures) of Protestant views of religion that are widespread in recent literature, the function of an immediate intuition of the universe as the criterion for defining religion and determining its ideal and corrupted forms still works to categorize much of what is taken to be religion as merely a corrupt form of religion. The point is relevant not only for the judgment of social, political, and economic arrangements in a transforming Germany but also for Europeans' encounters with people all over the world. Religion is not limited to immediate intuitions of the universe, but insofar as a proper connection to those intuitions is lost or outweighed by other factors, the relevant religious phenomena become attenuated or corrupt.

---

[25] See Dole, *Schleiermacher on Religion*, 80, and Schleiermacher's encompassing portrayal of the "religious phenomena of our time" (*On Religion*, 64–6).

G. W. F. HEGEL ON RELIGION'S FORM AND OBJECT

Schleiermacher's contemporary and rival, Hegel, offered a very different reconceptualization of religion in response to the social and intellectual upheavals of the era. Like Schleiermacher, Hegel sought to develop a distinctly modern account of religion that was responsive to these contemporary developments, but the contrasts between their views are vast and vibrantly illuminate the depth of contestation over the category of religion during this period. Hegel's transformation of the concept of religion is partially concealed by his claims that his own work does nothing more than transform the content of religion into philosophy, but it is no less dramatic.[26] On one hand, that claim suggests that he offers virtually nothing new—that the content of his philosophy was already widely available in Christianity. On the other hand, that claim is only possible for Hegel because of his accounts of the relation between religion and philosophy as well of Christianity. In part for this reason, the reconceptualization of religion is central to his project.

Hegel's mature conceptualization of religion can be usefully treated in terms of coordinated accounts of religion's form and its content, or object. Whereas Schleiermacher focused on religion's essential forms—intuition and feeling—and sharply limited what could be said about its content, Hegel gives form and content comparable weight. In Hegel's conception, religion and philosophy share a common object, the absolute; yet each has a different characteristic mode of cognizing this object. He begins his lectures on the philosophy of religion by drawing attention to the common object shared by religion and philosophy. For Hegel:

> it must be said that the content of philosophy, its need and interest, is wholly in common with that of religion. The object of religion, like that of philosophy, is the eternal truth, God and nothing but God and the explication of God. Philosophy is only explicating *itself* when it explicates religion, and when it explicates itself it is explicating religion. . . . Thus religion and philosophy coincide in one. In fact philosophy is itself the service of God, as is religion.[27]

---

[26] My interpretation of Hegel's philosophy of religion is, like all, controversial. I have developed my interpretation at length in Thomas A. Lewis, *Religion, Modernity, and Politics in Hegel* (Oxford: Oxford University Press, 2011).

[27] Hegel, *Lectures on the Philosophy of Religion*, 1:63–4.

Religion and philosophy are both efforts to grasp "the absolute," which religion has tended to express with the language of God. Crucially, however, at this point in Hegel's analysis, these terms—the absolute and God—function largely as placeholders. They are precisely what are being explicated, in part through these lectures and in part elsewhere in Hegel's philosophical system. To begin reading the lectures with a particular conception of God in mind and to take statements such as the quote above as evidence that Hegel is talking about that specific object (that "God") is to base one's interpretation on precisely the assumptions—particularly assumptions about the nature of religion and of God—that Hegel is calling into question and ultimately undermining.

This is precisely where attentiveness to the shifting conceptualization of religion—stressed in the work of scholars such as Masuzawa and Kippenberg—can contribute so much to the interpretation of the history of philosophy of religion. Carefully examining the manner in which Hegel reconceptualizes religion—not simply jumping into his descriptions of God, for instance—is essential to interpreting his philosophy of religion. Despite the grand tone of his language, all that Hegel has told us at this point is that religion and philosophy share a common object—that which is absolute—and that the task of the philosophy of religion, like philosophy more generally, is to explicate this object. The course of the lectures consists to a large degree of Hegel's exploration of just this point: he initially provides an abstract account of this object; then, in the second part of the lectures, examines how various forms of religion have conceived the absolute; and, finally, in his treatment of the "consummate religion," sketches the way the concept of religion (set out in part 1) is realized in Christianity—as Hegel interprets this authentic core of Christianity. Ultimately, Christianity reveals the absolute, spirit, as present in the community rather than simply standing over, above, or beyond the community. Thus, although we may have preconceptions about this object, only philosophy—which includes *philosophy* of religion—can provide an authoritative account of this content.

This distinctive role and authority of philosophy vis-à-vis religion is grounded in Hegel's account of the distinctive forms of religion and philosophy. Both are forms of cognition of the absolute, but each is dominated by a different form of cognition. For Hegel, religion is closely associated with representation (*Vorstellung*), which is characterized by images, metaphors, and narratives. While the most obvious forms of representation are sensible, as in the image of the tree of knowledge or the serpent, not all representations are sensible. Teachings such as that God created the cosmos are not sensible, since they involve the creation of time and space—not a story that takes place within time and space. What characterizes representation is thus not the sensible nature of images and most metaphors but the manner in which representation presents objects as freestanding or independent rather than existing in necessary relationship with each other. Its objects are marked by a givenness and particularity.[28] Philosophy, for Hegel, is distinguished by the purely conceptual form of thinking (*Denken*) that presents its objects in their necessary relations with each other. This form of cognition overcomes the arbitrariness of merely given content. Thinking can express the genuine content of representation and does so more adequately by virtue of abstracting from the stubborn givenness still present in the latter. In its narratives, for instance, religious representations portray necessary relations as arbitrary and contingent, the result of chance events such as the appearance of the serpent in the Garden of Eden. Thought, by contrast, is not limited by such finite, arbitrary constraints. Consequently, thinking, rather than representation provides the most adequate and authoritative account of the absolute.

Hegel's discussion of these forms of cognition in relation to religion builds and depends on the accounts of intuition, representation, and thought that he develops in his *Encyclopaedia of Philosophical Sciences* and related lectures.[29] As in the case of Schleiermacher, then, Hegel's reconceptualization is interconnected with his philosophical account of feeling, experience, and thought. We cannot adequately interpret this crucial episode in the history of religion's conceptualization without attending to the philosophical issues that are central to it. For Schleiermacher and Hegel, the conceptualization of religion depends upon their accounts of human feeling, cognition, and action. They thus make explicit what remains merely implicit in a great deal of theorizing of religion. Conceptions of the human subject—of our cognition as well as the relation between our practical and theoretical

---

[28] Hegel, *Lectures on the Philosophy of Religion*, 1:300–1.

[29] For the English translations, see G. W. F. Hegel, *Hegel's Philosophy of Mind*, trans. W. Wallace, A. V. Miller, and M. J. Inwood (Oxford: Clarendon Press, 2007), §§ 440–68, and G. W. F. Hegel, *Lectures on the Philosophy of Spirit 1827–8*, trans. Robert R. Williams (Oxford: Oxford University Press, 2007).

activity, for instance—are integral to conceptions of religion. In this respect, even theorizing of religion that seeks to abstain from these philosophical questions will draw upon particular sets of answers to them, whether conscious of doing so or not. Philosophy is thus unavoidable in the conceptualization of religion.

While Hegel at times downplays the dramatic nature of his claims about the authoritative character of philosophy vis-à-vis religion, the consequences are vast.[30] As much as Hegel's project seeks to validate inherited religious claims, it does so by justifying them as representations. Their genuine significance lies not in their relation to particular historical events or literalistic readings of the representational claims but in their representational expression of the truths treated most adequately in philosophy. In perhaps the most important example, Hegel preserves much traditional language about God, validating and justifying it; yet, over the course of his philosophical system, he argues that this absolute is to be understood in terms of the social practices of the human community rather than the super-human being frequently presented in religious representations. This philosophical insight, however, cannot be a starting point for the development of this knowledge. To the contrary, religion is a necessary stage in our learning and appropriation of these insights. Religion is more than a stepping stone to philosophy, yet it is the manner through which we first learn what philosophy ultimately teaches in a higher form. For Hegel, then, the term religion refers to the representations and other practices through which we come to know the absolute, which turns out to be our own essence, spirit.

In line with this important pedagogical role for religion, Hegel develops a vision in which religion plays a central role in shaping our deep intuitions about social and political life. Because religion shares philosophy's content but is more closely connected to feeling, religion—particularly a child's early religious formation—frequently powerfully informs the subject's most firmly held commitments about our relations to others—how we depend on them, what we

---

[30] Though it is beyond the scope of the present discussion, attention to Hegel's historical context—particularly to the political stakes of claims about religion, specifically those that challenge its role in legitimizing political authority—will shed much insight on Hegel's possible motives for downplaying these consequences. This is a further aspect of the turn to history that I am recommending. I have attended more closely to such issues in Lewis, *Religion, Modernity, and Politics in Hegel*, especially 17–25 and 98–106.

owe them, how we ought to act toward them, and so forth. While these commitments can in principle be revised, they are often deeply habitual and pre-reflective. They constitute what we take for granted (and do not articulate) as much as or more than views we espouse in words. Subsequent philosophical reflection may critique them and/or offer explicit justification for them. Depending on circumstances the result may be a reformation of habits or a divided self split between deeply ingrained habits and pre-reflective responses, on one hand, and explicit, theoretical commitments, on the other.

With respect to the conceptualization of religion, a crucial point is that religion will be closely connected to politics. Both social and political institutions, on one hand, and religion, on the other, manifest our conceptions of the communal social practices that collectively constitute spirit or the absolute. While Hegel distinguishes the two and argues adamantly against conceptions that would offer religious or theological legitimation for particular political claims, the two cannot be separated in the manner that Schleiermacher advocates.

CONCLUDING IMPLICATIONS

Even these brief accounts of Schleiermacher and Hegel point to the importance of the appropriate framing for investigations of crucial moments in the history of philosophy of religion. If we do not approach such figures with a broad enough lens, readings such as these are ruled out before we begin. If we rush to provide Hegel's account of God without situating it within the larger context of his account of religion, for instance, we easily overlook how dramatically he transforms the sense of terms such as "God" and "divine." Unconsciously importing more conventional meanings of these terms, we easily end up with a reading deeply at odds with his project. And to interpret his use of these terms properly, we need to begin with the role of religion in his larger project. Though the mistake might appear harder to make with respect to Schleiermacher, since the title of the second speech ("The Essence of Religion") seems to make explicit that he is treating the conceptualization of religion, that can make the danger more subtle. For in Schleiermacher's case, a proper appreciation of his broader conceptualization of religion requires distinguishing it from the narrower account of religion's essence: even within the 1799 *On Religion*, Schleiermacher's conceptualization of religion is not completed with the end of the second speech. While the point is crucial with regard to Schleiermacher and Hegel, a charitable hermeneutic requires that we assume many other thinkers are developing comparably transformative projects.

The differences between Schleiermacher's and Hegel's philosophies of religion, then, are not well captured by focusing on the differences in their conceptions of God or even their accounts of the relation between religion and belief. They do not simply offer alternative accounts of the paths toward and possibilities of knowing God; they disagree more profoundly about the form and content of religion as a whole. Although their divergent views of cognition are a crucial aspect of their differences, even a focus on this issue must appreciate that the phenomena to be analyzed, what each considers "religion," are very different. And the delineation of this object of inquiry, religion, will require articulating its relation to other concepts, such as philosophy, politics, the natural sciences, and so forth, with the understanding that these too are being reconceptualized during this period. Thus, if we seek to articulate questions to which they offer competing answers, we will need to frame the questions more broadly than we may be in the habit of doing and attend to the way that the questions themselves shift.

To learn as much as we can from and about these figures, then, we must approach them by asking how they conceive religion, not only by asking how they treat some particular object that we have already deemed to be religion. While the latter project—asking what Schleiermacher or Hegel have to say about a particular object that the investigator deems religion—is certainly a valid project, it should not be confused with or be allowed to obscure the distinct project of asking how they understand religion. Moreover, in most cases, discerning what they have to say about religion as defined by a particular interpreter will usually require attending to the ways in which they—Schleiermacher or Hegel, for instance—conceptualize religion. Only then will we be in a position to determine what they might have to say about the investigator's conception of God, for instance.

In closing, let me suggest three levels at which we might further pursue the consequences of focusing on this contestation over the concept of religion. In drawing attention to the centrality of debates over the concept of religion to the history of philosophy of religion,

I hope to situate the basic question, "What is religion?" at a central point in the field. While the points made in previous paragraphs might appear obvious and uncontroversial, making them central has significant implications. It reflects viewing this question as properly prior to classical questions about the existence of God, since it suggests not only that the object whose existence is being debated is far from a constant in the discussion but also that the import of the question is in flux. Moreover, the meaning and relative significance of questions about the justifiability of belief depend no less heavily on frequently transforming accounts of cognition and its pertinence to religion. Making "What is religion?" a, if not the, central question should therefore dislodge classical questions about the existence of God and the rationality of belief from the central place they have often occupied in philosophy of religion. Nonetheless, I do not want these questions to be abandoned. To the contrary, it is integral to my point that we will only be in a position to answer these questions well when they are situated within the broader context of religion's conceptualization. Only then can we avoid misreading historical figures as well as flattening our own constructive deliberations by presupposing conceptions of God and belief that have been and should continue to be subject to contentious debate. The encounter between a turn to history in philosophy of religion and a turn to the history of the study of religion—which has foregrounded the transformation in the conceptualization of religion—thus bears significant fruits for philosophy of religion itself.

Second, the discussion above implicitly points to the way that knowledge of our past—of the processes and developments through which we have come to pose the questions as we do—will profoundly shape our ongoing reflections. Developing this point fully would require more central attention than this chapter has given it; I have not here sought to work through the arguments of Taylor, Rorty, and Herdt about why historical studies matter, for instance. And the precise nature of the claim will depend on the epistemological views one endorses. Nonetheless, the investigations of Schleiermacher and Hegel above indicate that historical inquiry can do much to reveal hidden assumptions, expose the understructures of our arguments, and identify alternative paths. Turning to history, then, should be of more than "merely historical" interest. It bears directly on our contemporary constructive work. For this reason as well, history should figure prominently in philosophy of religion's future.

Finally, framing our investigation of central texts in the philosophy of religion in this manner illuminates the role that these works have had in determining the object of the study of religion, and thereby forming religious studies, in the first place. Whether we think of Kant's and Schleiermacher's influence on Rudolf Otto, Durkheim's relation to figures such as Kant and Hegel, or Schleiermacher's broader impact on our contemporary public discourse on religion, these looming figures from the philosophy of religion have shaped the course of much academic as well as public discourse on religion. As we seek to analyze this discourse and its history, we cannot do without the kind of careful interpretation, attentive to the conceptualization of religion, that scholars such as Dole offer. What might appear to be narrow, highly specialized studies of interest only to scholars of Schleiermacher, for instance, can have significant consequences for tracing the conceptualization of religion. In this case, Dole's interpretation necessitates important revisions to widespread contemporary narratives about the role of Protestant presuppositions in the formation of religious studies. And neither of the two major Protestant thinkers discussed in this chapter offers a view of religion as simply interior and only peripherally related to practice, society, and politics. More generally, the significance of important figures from the history of philosophy of religion extends far beyond the bounds of philosophy of religion, as becomes all the more apparent if we appreciate the extent to which they reframe the topic itself rather than viewing them simply as offering answers to narrower, predetermined questions.

Attending to the central role of contestations over the concept of religion in the philosophy of religion thus constitutes an important step toward moving philosophy of religion into closer conversation with other subfields of religious studies. It demonstrates what philosophers of religion have to contribute to broader debates about the category of religion. It not only uncovers their historical role in subsequent developments but also reveals the extent to which these later developments often turn upon underlying philosophical disagreements, whether concerning accounts of human cognition or of the relation between ritualized practices and the formation of belief. In other words, historical and social scientific studies of religion necessarily presuppose responses to the kinds of philosophical questions about the nature of reason, belief, and practice that lie at the heart of much work in philosophy of religion. Any attempt to theorize religion depends upon prior commitments—implicit or explicit—about how to construct the object that needs investigation. And these commitments involve non-trivial claims about the nature of reason and its relation to other, related forms of human sensibility. There is nothing wrong with such reliance, but it should be more than implicit. Turning the philosophy of religion toward its history—particularly toward transformative moments in that history—helps to bring that dependence to the surface.[31] By learning from other shifts toward history within religious studies, then, philosophy of religion can better articulate its ongoing significance for religious studies at a moment when important elements of the study of religion have turned more toward social scientific approaches. Demonstrating philosophy of religion's historical relation to broader, interdisciplinary discussions of the concept of religion thus illuminates the prominent role that philosophy of religion ought to continue to play in contemporary iterations of these debates.

---

[31] In particular, attending to the developments from Kant to Marx with attention to these issues will highlight the close relationship between philosophy of religion and the emergence of the sociology of religion.

4

Beyond Comparative Religious Ethics

Both participants and observers often conceive of "comparative religious ethics" as a distinct subfield within the larger field of religious ethics.[1] At times, it seems to be referred to as distinct from ethics proper, a kind of neighboring subfield rather than a part of ethics itself. This conception of comparative religious ethics as a distinct endeavor is driven by a number of factors, including books and conferences framed by this rubric, influential histories and typologies of the subfield, and paradigmatic, "double-barreled" studies that involve extensive, high-quality studies of two major figures or traditions.[2] All of these contributions have been important in advancing our understanding of the significance of comparative studies.

[1] For a particularly crisp example, see Sumner B. Twiss and Bruce Grelle, "Human Rights and Comparative Religious Ethics: A New Venue," *The Annual of the Society of Christian Ethics* 23 (1995): 21. For additional examples, see Elizabeth M. Bucar, "Methodological Invention as a Constructive Project: Exploring the Production of Ethical Knowledge through the Interaction of Discursive Logics," *Journal of Religious Ethics* 36, no. 3 (2008): 355; David Decosimo, "Comparison and the Ubiquity of Resemblance," *Journal of the American Academy of Religion* 78, no. 1 (2010): 227; and Irene Oh, *The Rights of God: Islam, Human Rights, and Comparative Ethics* (Washington, DC: Georgetown University Press, 2007), 2. Cf. John Kelsay, "Just War, Jihad, and the Study of Comparative Ethics," *Ethics & International Affairs* 24, no. 3 (2010): 228, and John Kelsay, "The Present State of the Comparative Study of Religious Ethics," *Journal of Religious Ethics* 40, no. 4 (2012): 583–602.

[2] I have in mind the series of conferences from 1986–1989 at Chicago Divinity School that produced three influential collections: Frank Reynolds and David Tracy, eds., *Myth and Philosophy* (Albany: State University of New York Press, 1990); *Discourse and Practice* (Albany: State University of New York Press, 1992); and *Religion and Practical Reason: New Essays in the Comparative Philosophy of Religions* (Albany: State University of New York Press, 1994). Prominent typologies are found in Robin W. Lovin and Frank Reynolds, "In the Beginning," in *Cosmogony and Ethical Order: New Studies in Comparative Ethics*, ed. Robin W. Lovin and Frank Reynolds

Nonetheless, I want to argue that the time has come to move beyond this model of comparative religious ethics—a model in which "CRE" is a distinct subfield typified by studies of two or more figures. Explicitly comparative studies should be encouraged, but CRE should not be a subfield. Rather, religious ethics as a whole should appreciate the fruits of this body of literature from the last several decades.[3] In particular, the insights developed from extensive methodological reflection on comparative ethics should permeate the field of religious ethics as a whole. Perhaps most significantly, we should recognize the extent to which all interpretation involves comparison as well as the import of the work done in the scholar's own mind. While such insights are not unique to comparative religious ethics, the preoccupation with the methodology of comparison, combined with worries about avoiding ethnocentrism, has placed these issues at the fore of recent theorizing of comparison. Conceiving of religious ethics as a whole along these lines opens the way for a more inclusive and encompassing vision of religious ethics—further undermining the hegemony of Christianity within the field of religious ethics. The result, as I imagine it, is a vision of religious ethics that engages a variety of traditions and brings that engagement into a common conversation. That conversation will initially be conducted with vocabulary and conceptual tools marked by a Western intellectual heritage, but it can and should be continually supplemented and expanded through encounters with materials from a wide range of other contexts.

(Chicago: University of Chicago Press, 1985), 1–35; Sumner B. Twiss, "Four Paradigms in Teaching Comparative Religious Ethics," in *Explorations in Global Ethics: Comparative Religious Ethics and Interreligious Dialogue*, ed. Sumner B. Twiss and Bruce Grelle (Boulder, CO: Westview Press, 1998), 11–33, and "Comparison in Religious Ethics," in *Blackwell Companion to Religious Ethics*, ed. William Schweiker, (Malden, MA: Blackwell, 2005), 147–55; and Bucar, "Methodological Invention." For paradigmatic comparative studies, see David Little and Sumner B. Twiss, *Comparative Religious Ethics: A New Approach* (San Francisco: Harper & Row, 1978); Lee H. Yearley, *Mencius and Aquinas: Theories of Virtue and Conceptions of Courage* (Albany: State University of New York Press, 1990); and Aaron Stalnaker, *Overcoming Our Evil: Human Nature and Spiritual Exercises in Xunzi and Augustine* (Washington, DC: Georgetown University Press, 2006), as well as two important recent works: Elizabeth M. Bucar, *Creative Conformity: The Feminist Politics of U.S. Catholic and Iranian Shi'i Women* (Washington, DC: Georgetown University Press, 2011) and David A. Clairmont, *Moral Struggle and Religious Ethics: On the Person as Classic in Comparative Theological Contexts* (Malden, MA: Wiley-Blackwell, 2011).

[3] Although I focus here on religious ethics, the claims at issue have bearing on other areas of religious studies and beyond.

To make this case, I will discuss several of the most significant results that I believe should be gleaned from this work on the methodology of comparison. I then turn to rationales offered for comparative studies of ethics in order to consider whether these justify CRE as a distinct subfield. Finally, I offer a more developed account of this vision for the field of religious ethics as a whole.

THE FRUITS OF METHODOLOGICAL REFLECTION ON COMPARISON

Before moving into the body of my argument, I want to briefly note a few points that I believe can be taken for granted in the wake of recent scholarship on comparison in ethics. These points should also make more apparent the kinds of material I have in mind when I refer to comparative religious ethics. First, although some people still think of entire religions, such as Christianity or Buddhism, as possible objects of comparison, I think we have learned far too much about the diversity within traditions to believe that comparisons framed in terms of "Buddhism and Christianity" or "Judaism and Islam" will be very fruitful. Religious traditions are too vast and internally diverse to constitute particularly productive objects of comparison. Some generalizations may be possible; and there may be cases where such generalizations are illuminating. Most often, however, such attempts allow one particular manifestation of the tradition—not infrequently the author's own and/or a caricature of the other—to represent the tradition as a whole; most such scholarship fails to take seriously some of the most basic insights of the field of religious studies.

Accordingly, the most fruitful comparative studies have been and will be those that have much more focused comparanda, such as texts, individuals, or relatively localized communities. Only in this manner can comparative studies achieve the level of scholarship expected of other scholars of religion. And only in this way can comparative studies respond to the accusations of superficiality that are often leveled against them.[4]

---

[4] Stalnaker puts these issues very well; *Overcoming Our Evil*, 14–15.

Second, I take for granted that "religious ethics" should not simply be a politically correct way of saying "Christian ethics" or "Christian and Jewish ethics." Studies of figures, texts, and communities from other religions belong in religious ethics just as much as studies of Christian and Jewish materials. Although this point should be obvious, I make it explicit in order to make sure that "comparative religious ethics" does not, even inadvertently, become a kind of code for studies of "others," which implies that "religious ethics" (without qualifier) actually consists in studies of Christianity and Judaism.[5] If we are to move fully beyond an assumption of Christianity or perhaps Christianity and Judaism as the implicit norm or center of religious studies, "comparative" cannot simply refer to studies of anything other than these.[6]

A third point begins to move us into the fruits of these debates over comparative religious ethics. Here, I largely take for granted, as a starting point for my argument, the abandonment of aspirations to universality. More specifically, comparative ethical studies should not be understood as aiming toward the discovery of significant, specific ethical views or claims that are actually common to all religions. To be clear, my point here concerns the discovery of a preexisting universality. I am not making a claim about whether any particular ethical view might be universally true; nor am I commenting on the possibility of bringing about such commonality over time. But we have already found too much diversity among religious views around the world to expect to find that these differences could all be judged superficial. Even allowing for the possibility of discovering some commonalities, we must recognize that these will inevitably be encountered together with important differences. Focusing exclusively on commonalities easily blinds us to what can be learned from these differences. The most important comparative work seems to have gone well beyond being fundamentally oriented around looking for similarities.

The point about universality cuts deeper, however: it concerns not simply the conclusions but also the structure of arguments.

---

[5] I discuss issues of who "we" are and "others" at greater length below.

[6] One other point that I take for granted in this context is that, as a component of the academic study of religion, religious ethics should not be understood fundamentally as the investigation and elaboration of ethics from the point of view of "one's own" tradition. It will include work fitting this description, but this account should not be seen as describing the field as a whole.

Comparison should not presuppose a universal framework for comparison or any sort of basic structure common to all ethical discourses. Perhaps ironically, just such a goal was central to the works that are often taken to have initiated the field. This point, then, moves us into methodological debates that have been central to the field. As a number of histories of comparative religious ethics argue, the field in some sense began in 1978, with the publication of Ronald Green's *Religious Reason: The Rational and Moral Basis of Religious Belief* and David Little and Sumner Twiss's *Comparative Religious Ethics: A New Approach.*[7] Green seeks to ground the possibility and procedures of comparison in a deep structure of moral reasoning that, he contends, is universal, even if the content of the structure is developed differently in different traditions.[8] Little and Twiss seek to be more open to a variety of conceptions of moral reason—in part through claiming to establish the structures of reasoning empirically rather than a priori— but nonetheless develop a general structure of moral argumentation that is meant to provide the framework for all comparisons. Thus, whereas Robin Lovin and Frank Reynolds influentially label Green's approach formalist, they label Little's and Twiss's semi-formal.[9]

While these early projects were centered on establishing universal structures that would enable comparison, much subsequent work in comparative religious ethics has been more preoccupied with the depth of differences. Jeffrey Stout influentially critiqued Little and Twiss's work for presupposing a universality to the structure of practical justification.[10] Lovin and Reynolds' 1985 edited volume, *Cosmogony and Ethical Order: New Studies in Comparative Ethics,* decisively shaped subsequent discussion by foregrounding concerns

---

[7] For such histories and related typologies, see Thomas A. Lewis, "Vergleichende Ethik in Nordamerika: Methodologische Probleme und Ansätze [expanded and updated]," in *Wertetraditionen und Wertekonflikte: Ethik in Zeiten der Globalisierung,* ed. Gabriele Münnix (Nordhausen: Verlag Traugott Bautz, 2013), 321–35; Bucar, "Methodological Invention"; Kelsay, "Just War, Jihad"; and William Schweiker, "Responsibility and Comparative Ethics," in *Power, Value, and Conviction: Theological Ethics in the Postmodern Age* (Cleveland: Pilgrim Press, 1998). For a treatment attentive to earlier precedents, see Twiss "Comparison in Religious Ethics."

[8] Ronald Michael Green, *Religious Reason: The Rational and Moral Basis of Religious Belief* (Oxford: Oxford University Press, 1978) and *Religion and Moral Reason: A New Method for Comparative Study* (Oxford: Oxford University Press, 1988).

[9] Lovin and Reynolds, "In the Beginning."

[10] Jeffrey Stout, "Weber's Progeny, Once Removed," *Religious Studies Review* 6, no. 4 (1980): 289–95, and *Democracy and Tradition* (Princeton: Princeton University Press, 2004), 285.

about the complex and varied ways in which ethical views are inter-connected with cosmogonies.[11] We cannot necessarily separate an individual's or a group's ethical views from their metaphysical views for the sake of comparing their ethics alone. Greater attention to the historical particularity and the embeddedness of ethical views in complex religious and philosophical conceptions is needed.

Although some take this importance of historical specificity to undermine the possibility of comparison, this need not follow. Rather, I take the point to be that there is no universal formula for the relation between ethical claims and cosmological views. In some cases, on some questions, these considerations will be inseparable; in others they will not. This variability means that one cannot simply ignore the question of whether a group of ethical claims can be understood independently of a larger cosmological vision, but neither should we presuppose that this connection is in every case of such a character that meaningful comparison is impossible. Without a universal formula or method for comparison, whether particular comparisons will be possible as well as fruitful will depend on specifics of the comparison.

With this point, we arrive at one of the most significant methodo-logical results of recent reflection of comparison. Deeply influenced by the concerns placed in the foreground by Lovin and Reynolds, much subsequent work in the area has tended to reject the universal-istic presuppositions of projects such as Green's and, therewith, the idea that the basic categories of analysis—or the forms of reason—can be established independently of the objects of inquiry without risking seriously hindering our interpretation of those objects. Without a universal structure for comparison, the onus for the legitimacy of the comparison comes to fall on the categories or concepts through which the comparanda are brought together and compared. Of course, in some sense we can ask any question we want of a text, but if one of the goals of comparison is to appreciate the way that a text or thinker conceptualizes the topic itself, that will require framing the inquiry in a manner that can be sensitive to deep differences in the crucial concepts operative in various texts (or other materials).[12]

---

[11] Robin W. Lovin and Frank Reynolds, eds., *Cosmogony and Ethical Order: New Studies in Comparative Ethics* (Chicago: University of Chicago Press, 1985).

[12] Such sensitivity does not, however, imply being uncritical; I return to this issue below.

Broadly speaking, the goals have been to conceive of categories of comparison such that they simultaneously appreciate the particularity of the comparanda and allow us to see certain commonalities; they must be sufficiently relevant to both objects of comparison to enable comparison while also aiding us in appreciating the differences.

The efforts to think through the categories of comparison in a manner that moves beyond these general goals have been multiple. Lee Yearley's path-breaking *Mencius and Aquinas* identifies "one of the most central and vexing problems in comparative studies . . . [as] the choice of which categories to employ when we do comparisons and how best to use them."[13] He responds to this challenge with "[t]he notion that analogical terms have systematically related focal and secondary meaning . . . ."[14] Focal meanings—of terms such as virtue or courage—orient the inquiry and serve as a starting point for the encounter between objects. Through the comparison itself, the meaning of a term can be extended analogically into secondary meanings that capture a concept operating in one of the objects under study. His focus on analogical terms and the distinction between focal and secondary meanings seeks to draw connections while safeguarding differences—avoiding reducing meanings to singularity, as univocal understandings of terms would. Yearley highlights that he "*initially deriv[es] the focal meaning of most key terms from contemporary English usage; that is, from my understanding of the terms.*"[15] Although the focal meanings of key terms are—crucially—revised during the process of comparison itself, they originate from the scholar's "home discourse."[16] The sources for the meanings of key terms are not only the objects of comparison but also the comparative scholar's home context. This focus on the decisive role of the scholar's own intellectual context in shaping the categories of comparison will be significantly further developed—and complicated—in later comparative work, such as that of Stalnaker and Schofer.

More recently, Aaron Stalnaker has theorized the categories of comparison in terms of "bridge concepts." These are "general ideas, such as 'virtue' and 'human nature,' which can be given enough

---

[13] Yearley, *Mencius and Aquinas*, 190.
[14] Yearley, *Mencius and Aquinas*, 190.
[15] Yearley, *Mencius and Aquinas*, 190, emphasis in original. Regarding revision, see especially 193.
[16] Yearley, *Mencius and Aquinas*, 191.

content to be meaningful and guide comparative inquiry yet are still open to greater specification in particular cases."[17] Whereas in Yearley's account of comparison the focal meanings of key terms come from the scholar's own native usage and are then extended analogically, Stalnaker's bridge concepts are intended to provide "thinner" concepts that are neutral vis-à-vis significant points of difference between the objects of comparison.[18] The study will then consist to a large degree in articulating the way that each thinker fills out the "thin" concept with which the analysis begins. They are meant to be specific enough to guide inquiry yet open-ended enough to provide space for—rather than occlude—the particular questions and theories through which individual figures have developed their accounts of these concepts.[19] The bridge concepts may or may not correspond directly to specific terms in the materials being compared, but they are open to revision on the basis of engagement with the objects of study. The bridge concepts are developed inductively, on the basis of the preliminary stages of the investigation (which occur well before the writing of the book begins). They emerge, at least in part, from the scholar's initial engagement with the materials and are intended for a given comparison, not as "hypotheses about transcultural universals."[20] Yet they may also be profoundly shaped by other contemporary scholarship. Stalnaker's bridge concept of "spiritual exercises" is initially elaborated largely in terms of the recent work of Pierre Hadot.[21] Although Hadot's work treats the intellectual context out of which Augustine emerged, this commonality is not essential to the role that Hadot plays in the articulation of the bridge concept. To the contrary, Hadot's role in the formation of Stalnaker's own, evolving understanding of the concept appears more important. The point is emphatically not that Stalnaker simply uncritically takes over contemporary categories that are ready to hand. It is, rather, that the ongoing process through which the bridge concepts are elaborated is crucially shaped by the scholar's own intellectual formation, not

---

[17] Stalnaker, *Overcoming Our Evil*, 17.

[18] Stalnaker, *Overcoming Our Evil*, 48.

[19] "[B]ridge concepts are designed to elicit theoretical formulations in each object compared (i.e., their 'vocabulary'), including questions and basic orientations, but to refrain from reshaping the terms each thinker uses into some fundamentally new form" (Stalnaker, *Overcoming Our Evil*, 18).

[20] Stalnaker, *Overcoming Our Evil*, 17.

[21] Stalnaker, *Overcoming Our Evil*, 40–3.

simply by the objects of comparison. The scholar's own standpoint plays an essential role in the process.

Elizabeth Bucar's important reflections on her own process of elaborating the concepts through which she would carry out her comparative project are particularly illuminating: they demonstrate the way that these concepts or categories are developed through engagement with the material under study as well as reflection on the scholar's own intellectual background and context. As Stalnaker and Jonathan Schofer note, this process is often largely hidden from the reader of the finished project.[22] Bucar's piece has the great virtue of making this process itself visible. Early in her article, she notes the strong focus on categories of comparison in what she identifies as the "third wave" of comparative religious ethics. Building on this attention to categories, she argues that the categories being used in a number of these third-wave projects were proving inadequate in her attempts to negotiate her objects of study. Her larger project (which comes to fruition in her subsequent book *Creative Conformity*), examines U.S. Catholic and Iranian Shi'i women. Reflecting back on her own work on the project, she observes that she quickly encountered the need for categories beyond those highlighted by other third-wave authors or provided by either more secular feminist ethics or Muslim ethics. Her language is revealing: "the questions my data posed to me early on. . . . "[23] The need for adequate categories arose through engagement with her materials, not simply by virtue of an abstract procedure. Important contributions by other feminist legal scholars and philosophers (e.g., Rebecca Cook, Julie Stone Peters, Martha Nussbaum, and Susan Moller Okin) were inadequate for her purposes:

> because my concern with feminist ethics was simply different. I was not interested in constructing a common feminist morality or in moral judgments of specific religious norms or practices; instead, I wanted to describe and explain the specific ways Catholic and Shii women's discursive practices locate, reproduce, and shift moral knowledge within in local religious communities. . . . A central methodological question

---

[22] Stalnaker, *Overcoming Our Evil*, 32–3, and Jonathan W. Schofer, *Confronting Vulnerability: The Body and the Divine in Rabbinic Ethics* (Chicago: University of Chicago Press, 2010), 6.

[23] Bucar, "Methodological Invention," 362.

became: how can *religious piety*, as opposed to legal, sociological or political frameworks, function as the primary ground for comparison?[24]

Thus, what concepts or categories could enable the analysis and comparison of these materials without simply prejudging critical issues? Bucar repeatedly stresses the importance of her "data, which comprised writings by, and interviews with, public intellectuals in each religious community" and notes that her focus on clerical rhetoric emerged from her interviews with the women.[25] But this did not involve simply taking over their categories, seeking to understand them "on their own terms." As clerical rhetoric emerged as an important concept for her analysis, she sought out other sources that would give her tools for analyzing their rhetoric: Aristotle, Stephen Toulmin, and Chaïm Perelman. Her recounting of her own path brings out vividly the need for such concepts for the sake of analysis and comparison, their not being in any sense self-evident, and the way that they emerge and develop through engagement with both the objects of comparison and other resources the scholar brings to bear. These concepts are neither established a priori nor taken uncritically from the objects of comparison.[26]

---

[24] Bucar, "Methodological Invention," 362, emphasis in original.

[25] Bucar, "Methodological Invention," 363. Though one might raise questions regarding the way that Bucar circumscribes each of these communities, that issue does not threaten the more general point I am making here.

[26] The development and transformation of these categories through the process of comparison itself, highlighted by Yearley, Stalnaker, and Bucar, also illuminates what David Decosimo's treatment of comparison occludes. Decosimo distinguishes three different activities to which comparison may refer. The second and third are the most important here: the second "is a capacity implicit in and necessary for concept use. All concept use at some level requires a kind of quasi-comparison" ("Comparison and the Ubiquity of Resemblance," 228). Decosimo wants to distinguish this ordinary use of concepts from another sense of comparison, which he takes to be the comparison at issue in "comparative religious ethics." This activity "involves mastering the circumstances and consequences of application of a number of particular concepts such as *similarity, difference, resemblance, likeness*, and so on" (228–9). The problem here is that—as each of the authors above highlight—comparison frequently requires innovation and transformation in the way that concepts are used. One could say that much of the most important work in comparative studies takes place in the interstices between what he labels the second and third senses of comparison. Decosimo's use of Robert Brandom's work should provide him with the resources to make precisely this point, but he does not take the opportunity to do so. Rather, Decosimo's formulation of the second kind of comparison does not fully appreciate the extent to which comparison can challenge and change our normal use of categories, and his attempt to clarify the situation by distinguishing these three activities of comparison leaves us without the tools or perspective to appreciate this aspect of what takes place

Despite their differences, all of these efforts emerge from the understanding that the categories in terms of which we analyze material profoundly shape the interpretation of that material and that some of the most significant differences among the materials we are comparing concern the nature of the most basic concepts. Yet none of these approaches rest satisfied with simply attempting to understand the material "on its own terms." In the first place, such an attempt is called up short by the demands of comparison itself. Some common categories are necessary to enable comparison between figures employing different basic terms. For those who are suspicious of comparison, the obvious response is, "so much the worse for comparison." Close attention to the categories of comparison, however, reveals the inadequacy of this response. The problem lies in the deeper incoherence of the notion of understanding material simply "on its own terms." As much as work in comparative ethics has demonstrated the importance of strong philological and historical training, attention to the methodology of comparison brings out the extent to which attempts to understand others "on their own terms" typically occlude the vital function of the categories and preconceptions that the scholar brings to the encounter. Thus, attempts to avoid the perils of comparison by avoiding comparison altogether and treating the other on its own typically risk the greater danger of unknowingly distorting the other through the unconscious imposition of our concepts and categories.

Precisely on these matters comparative work in religious ethics has something to teach religious ethics as a whole. The concerns about the categories and concepts in terms of which material is analyzed are no more relevant to studies of more than one object than they are to studies of one. They are not unique to explicitly comparative projects. Thus, the broader import of the work just discussed is not simply that the categories to use are not obvious when comparing A with B (as in, Xunzi with Augustine) but, perhaps more profoundly, that the categories are never obvious, that every interpreter who seeks to understand another faces a comparable challenge. Any attempt to interpret another—whether from near or far—requires making that object

in many comparative projects. In other words, his formulation of the third kind of comparison as involving a distinct set of skills does not appreciate how much of the same kind of comparison is already taking place in the relatively ordinary use of concepts. I am grateful to Stephen Bush for helping me think through these issues.

comprehensible to me, either through expressing it in terms I already understand or through enabling me to understand terms (or senses of terms) that I previously could not. Thus, the theoretical issues involved are not *qualitatively* different when Stalnaker seeks to compare Xunzi and Augustine than when a scholar writes a study of "just" Xunzi or "just" Augustine. To make this claim is in no way to downplay the accomplishment represented by being able to conduct first-rate scholarship on figures from two very different contexts—such as Xunzi and Augustine. Yet one of the most significant fruits of the extensive theorizing of such comparison is that the theoretical challenges that are so obvious in comparative projects of that sort are no less present—even if they are far less apparent—in studies that engage only one figure.

One might hope to avoid the challenges of this kind of focus on categories through a study of one object (e.g., Augustine's thought) that draws on everyday words that are substantially underdetermined in their meanings. Thus, rather than having to develop bridge concepts or something comparable to bring together Xunzi's and Augustine's accounts of human nature, one might simply examine Augustine's elaboration of *caritas* by using rough translational equivalents, with the understanding that the determination of the meaning of those terms (such as "love") will be controlled by Augustine's work. In this way, the object under study—in this case Augustine's work—would provide the only elaboration of the concept, and we could study the inferential relations that give that concept its content in Augustine's thought. The conceptual challenges regarding the categories of analysis would presumably thereby be avoided, since we would not be comparing Augustine's (developed) account with some other account (even our own). Yet this approach assumes that the English terms used are sufficiently indeterminate in our linguistic community that they do virtually no substantive work in the analysis of Augustine's thought—that they are neutral vis-à-vis various possible ways of conceptualizing the content, e.g., Augustine's *caritas*. Although it is significant to note that certain terms are used in relatively diverse ways—and are thus relatively indeterminate in their content—even this *relative* indeterminacy may contain (often without our being conscious thereof) presuppositions at odds with those of the material being examined. What appears indeterminate and thus inclusive today may appear more determinate and non-neutral when considering material from substantially different times and places. Though this may not always be the case, only the critical interrogation of the categories of analysis can determine whether it is in any particular instance. Thus, even this strategy does not avoid the methodological challenges highlighted by reflection on comparison.[27]

To avoid misunderstanding, two points merit emphasis here. First, to stress the significance of these concepts or categories is in no way to suggest that attention to the categories of analysis should trade off with or substitute for attention to history. While some might see the preoccupation of some scholars of comparison with the categories of comparison as counting against or even replacing attention to history, there is no reason that should be the case.[28] Moreover, my focus on issues emerging from discussions of methodology should not suggest that I advocate some distinctive technique or method for comparative studies. For these reasons, I appreciate Scott Davis's point that "[t]here is . . . no substitute for history and ethnography. If the pursuit of method short circuits the history and ethnography, by providing categories and cubbyholes in which to file and dismiss the counter-intuitive, it is a positive danger to good work."[29] Yet part of what has been learned from this reflection on comparison is that the categories of analysis are no less an issue in doing history. Davis provides an illuminating example in a telling footnote where he suggests a line of

---

[27] I am deeply grateful to Stephen Bush for emphasizing this issue and helping me to think through it.

[28] John Kelsay and Jung Lee have both criticized the work of a number of authors discussed here for failing to attend adequately to issues of social context and power. Both express concern that a focus on notions of the self or anthropology has contributed to treating individuals as isolated. See John Kelsay, "Response to Papers for 'Ethnography, Anthropology, and Comparative Religious Ethics' Focus," *Journal of Religious Ethics* 38, no. 3 (2010): 487–92, and Jung H. Lee, "The Rhetoric of Context," *Journal of Religious Ethics* 41, no. 4 (2013): 574–5. While particular studies may have neglected attention to social contexts and power, I see nothing in a focus on philosophical or religious anthropology that need lead in this direction; to the contrary, it may well lead to an emphasis on the role of social forces in forming the subject. My own work on Hegel has been driven largely by these concerns; see, in particular, Thomas A. Lewis, *Freedom and Tradition in Hegel: Reconsidering Anthropology, Ethics, and Religion* (Notre Dame, IN: University of Notre Dame Press, 2005), 54–9 and 135–46.

[29] G. Scott Davis, "Two Neglected Classics of Comparative Ethics," *Journal of Religious Ethics* 36, no. 3 (2008): 398. See also his further elaboration of this view in G. Scott Davis, *Believing and Acting: The Pragmatic Turn in Comparative Religion and Ethics* (Oxford: Oxford University Press, 2012). Schofer has also argued powerfully for the relevance of ethnography to work in ethics; Jonathan W. Schofer, "Embodiment and Virtue in a Comparative Perspective," *Journal of Religious Ethics* 35, no. 4 (2007): 715–28.

criticism of Benjamin Schwartz's interpretation of Confucius: "This is neither the time nor the place to develop a critique of Schwartz, but if I am right about Fingarette and Douglas, then he should be seen as illustrating the consequences of doing history with questionable Western philosophical and psychological presuppositions."[30] Even in a study such as Schwartz's of the intellectual world of early China (where it is not treated explicitly comparatively), the concepts and other presuppositions that are brought to bear do much to shape the investigation.

Second, to claim that reflection on comparison brings these issues to the fore is not to claim that it is unique in doing so. The issues take on practical urgency in comparative studies, but the same concerns about the significance of the interpreter's own presuppositions (including concepts and categories) have been central to the concerns of a wide range of scholars theorizing interpretation. The hermeneutic tradition as well as American pragmatism offer many examples.[31] My point is that reflection on comparison has powerfully brought these issues to the fore, not that it is uniquely qualified or empirically unique in doing so.

The work of Jonathan Schofer places in relief the value of engagement with these discussions of comparison even for studies that focus principally on one text or body of material. His work demonstrates what attention to these concerns—so prominent in reflection on comparison—can and should bring to studies focused on one object rather than two or more. *The Making of a Sage* focuses on *The Fathers According to Rabbi Nathan*, while his second book, *Confronting Vulnerability*, engages a broader range of rabbinic materials. Neither work constitutes the kind of double-barreled comparative study typified by Yearley, Stalnaker, and Bucar. In both cases, however, Schofer devotes significant attention early in the work to the elaboration of the concepts that structure his project. In what he describes as "a theoretically informed descriptive analysis," he is self-conscious about these concepts and does not seek to confine the analysis to

---

[30] Davis, "Two Neglected Classics," 379 n. 4.

[31] Scott Davis's excellent *Believing and Acting* develops many related points through an examination of the tradition of American pragmatism. I consider his work to be a vital contribution to thinking through the issue of comparison in a way that shares many of my concerns and conclusions.

terms set by the materials themselves.[32] In the case of one of the most central terms framing his analysis, ethics, he writes, "Since there is no classical rabbinic term that corresponds with ethics in the full scope that the word has today, any account of rabbinic ethics requires an encounter between ancient texts and contemporary theory. I make that encounter explicit."[33] Even in cases where a related term can be found in the rabbinic materials, Schofer recognizes the need to elaborate the concepts explicitly. Thus, he realizes that interpreting these materials for us requires explicit attention to the concepts, not simply mimicking those found in the texts. He goes on to elaborate notions such as self and subject formation in relation to recent theoretical work including that of Alasdair MacIntyre, Paul Ricoeur, and Michel Foucault.[34] As in the works discussed above, however, the concepts are not simply established by these contemporary theorists but rather by "an ongoing jostling between texts and theory," which can only be partially reflected in the written text.[35] Crucial here—and concisely highlighting the broader significance of these reflections on comparison—is the final sentence of the quote above: "I make this encounter explicit." The encounter is taking place in any attempt to interpret; what Schofer learns from reflection on comparison is to make it explicit. In doing so, he brings out the profound significance of this history of reflection on the categories of comparison: it is equally relevant for seemingly "non-comparative" endeavors.

Focusing on the concepts and categories with which the scholar works also highlights the active work on the part of the interpreter. The scholar comparing is not simply a bystander, observing the materials encountering each other. Rather, the encounter is itself produced by the scholar. To take Stalnaker's case, not only did Xunzi and Augustine never encounter each other directly; more significantly, had they the opportunity to sit down with each other, the resulting dialogue would undoubtedly be very different from the

---

[32] Jonathan W. Schofer, *The Making of a Sage: A Study in Rabbinic Ethics* (Madison: University of Wisconsin Press, 2005), 7. Schofer's notion of "descriptive ethics" raises further issues that need not be addressed in the present context.

[33] Schofer, *Making of a Sage*, 9.

[34] Schofer, *Making of a Sage*, 11–22. See also Jonathan W. Schofer, "Self, Subject, and Chosen Subjection: Rabbinic Ethics and Comparative Possibilities," *Journal of Religious Ethics* 33, no. 2 (2005): 255–91. For comparable strategies in Schofer, *Confronting Vulnerability*, see 3–19.

[35] Schofer, *Confronting Vulnerability*, 6.

encounter produced by the scholar. This gap, however, reflects not (principally) the scholar's inability to reach a goal toward which she should be aspiring (predicting what such an encounter would have looked like) but rather that much of the power of a comparison (be it weak or great) derives not simply from the objects of comparison themselves but from the scholar's work bringing them together.[36] More specifically, the comparison is itself constituted by the scholar's active role in relating the objects through the categories of comparison. If we think of the categories of comparison in terms of questions, then the point is that the comparison is constituted by the questions asked no less than the objects of which they are asked. Yearley puts this point well in saying that "[t]he light produced . . . [in the comparison] is one that we ourselves cast."[37]

Yearley arguably represents a strong version of this claim, with his emphasis on the role of the scholar's own "analogical imagination."[38] He spends significant time defending the imagination's vital role in drawing connections through analogically extending the meanings of terms to encompass material coming from a different context. His point is not that this is an entirely freeform process, without standards, but he highlights that "the locus of comparison must exist in the scholar's mind and not in the objects studied."[39] It requires skills, such as radically questioning what one takes for granted, that the figures being studied may or may not have possessed. Moreover, Yearley's treatment of imagination also emphasizes the extent to which the scholar him- or herself can be transformed through the act of comparison.[40]

---

[36] The point brings to mind an important conclusion of Brent Sockness's study of Ernst Troeltsch and Wilhelm Hermann. After exhaustively examining both authors' explicit discussions of each other's works, he concludes that "as hermeneutical keys to each other's theological accomplishments, both predominant patterns of interpretation are deficient and misleading"; Brent W. Sockness, *Against False Apologetics: Wilhelm Hermann and Ernst Troeltsch in Conflict* (Tübingen: Mohr Siebeck, 1998), 206. That is, what Sockness's study reveals about the relationships between their thought is more profound and illuminating than what their actual encounters (both written and spoken) produced.

[37] Yearley, *Mencius and Aquinas*, 198.

[38] Yearley, *Mencius and Aquinas*, 197. Of course, the term "analogical imagination" derives from David Tracy, *The Analogical Imagination: Christian Theology and the Culture of Pluralism* (New York: Crossroad, 1981).

[39] Yearley, *Mencius and Aquinas*, 198. For further elaboration of his account of imagination, see 199–201.

[40] David Clairmont concludes his recent book with a comparable point about imagination and the transformation of the comparer (*Moral Struggle and Religious*

Whether or not one conceives of the scholar's activity in terms of imagination, however, these methodological reflections on comparison highlight the scholar's active role in any interpretive act. Analysis of a text does not happen on its own but rather depends on the scholar's interpretive skills and her engagement of them.[41] The point may seem obvious; in some sense it is. Yet the crucial implication here is that this is just as much the case whether one is explicitly comparing two figures from very different contexts, analyzing a single historical figure who has powerfully influenced one's own intellectual context, or studying a single figure from a culturally distant context. Each of these involves the active work of the scholar that the theorizing of comparison makes explicit.

In some sense, these points are the most obvious examples of the yields of theorizing comparison that are no less relevant to studies that are not explicitly comparative. Another factor is more implicit than explicit in these texts. The point about the way that the categories of comparison are themselves transformed through the comparative inquiry is in some sense only the tip of the iceberg with regard to the scholar's transformation. Much talk about comparison—by practitioners as well as observers—discusses the motives for, the challenges of, and the value of learning about other cultures. David Clairmont is most emphatic about this point, beginning his book with the question, "*What is it that finally drives us from the intellectual and social comforts of our own religious traditions to learn about what is unknown, and what might even prove to be irreconcilably different?*"[42] Despite important differences (to which I will return), even Stalnaker's presentation of "global neighborliness" as a motive

---

Ethics, 208). Jennifer Rapp seems to offer an even "stronger" version of this claim than Yearley's, arguing that "a comparison is more like a poem than a scientific hypothesis or logical argument"; Jennifer R. Rapp, "A Poetics of Comparison: Euripides, Zhuangzi, and the Human Poise of Imaginative Construction," *Journal of the American Academy of Religion* 78, no. 1 (2010): 164. One need not accept this sort of "strong" version of the claim, however, to appreciate the more general point about the significance of the activity in the scholar's mind. And this need not be understood as any more "subjective" than other forms of humanistic inquiry. Thus, while I share some of Jung Lee's concerns about the role of poeticization in recent work by Yearley and by Rapp, I do not see these problems as implicating other recent work with which Lee associates them.

[41] William Schweiker's discussion of interpretation as an activity also brings out this point ("Responsibility and Comparative Ethics," 113).

[42] Clairmont, *Moral Struggle and Religious Ethics*, 1, emphasis in original.

and goal of comparative studies can be read as conceiving comparison as "us" encountering one or more "others."[43] Though both authors qualify this point to some extent, this framing—comparison for the sake of learning about the "other"—continues to be influential.

I suspect, however, that a crucial aspect of what we are seeing in the last few decades of scholarship on these topics is that this us–other conception is being radically qualified—even if only implicitly. We can see this at a couple of levels: First, scholars such as Stalnaker, Bucar, and Clairmont have been deeply involved in careful studies of materials from very different contexts since early in their education. Their own intellectual formation is undoubtedly profoundly marked by materials from both of these contexts—in ways that exceed their awareness. It is hard to imagine for any of these thinkers that they had a "fully" developed concept of "human nature" (Stalnaker), "clerical rhetoric" (Bucar), or the "person" (Clairmont), prior to their engagements with Xunzi, Iranian Shi'i women, or Buddhaghosa, respectively. Their encounters and engagements with these materials are essential to their "own," "native" understanding, categories, and concepts. In Stalnaker's more recent work on the articulation of virtue, for instance, part of what we see is the extent to which his own, most central thinking about virtue is informed by his reading of early Chinese materials just as much as anything else.[44] For such scholars in particular, it is no longer adequate to think of their work in terms of their "own" intellectual identities (whether understood as modern/postmodern Western, Catholic, and/or secular) encountering some others. The point, to be sure, is not to downplay the differences between contemporary intellectual and cultural contexts and those of some of the figures being studied. It is, however, to recognize that despite these distances, the encounters across these distances have deeply shaped these scholars. That is one of the crucial—though to date still largely implicit—lessons of the points that various scholars have made about the transformative impact of comparison.[45]

---

[43] See Stalnaker, *Overcoming Our Evil*, xiii–xiv.

[44] Aaron Stalnaker, "Virtue as Mastery in Early Confucianism," *Journal of Religious Ethics* 38, no. 3 (2010): 404–28.

[45] Yearley, *Mencius and Aquinas*, 197–9; Clairmont, *Moral Struggle and Religious Ethics*, 190–209; and Bucar, "Methodological Invention," 2008.

Viewed in this light, Clairmont's repeated focus on "one's own tradition" (note the number of times the words "tradition" and "community" occur in his book's introduction alone) comes to appear as at least in part a defense mechanism, working to assure other Catholics that he is genuinely Catholic.[46] I take the brief invocation of MacIntyre on the final page to be quite telling. Precisely in MacIntyre's conception of second first languages, we see the reification of traditions as radically separate, even within one individual.[47] Perhaps Clairmont has drunk too deeply from MacIntyrean wells: by accepting such a MacIntyrean framing, Clairmont soft pedals the transformative impact of comparison that he otherwise seeks to highlight. Even his own Catholicism is presented in reified juxtaposition with the thought of Buddhaghosa. Moreover, he seems to accept and perhaps inadvertently promote an understanding of our contemporary historical situation as one in which most individuals are comfortably ensconced in a single, clearly defined tradition and in which encounters with "others" are voluntary, as his opening question implies.

Yet this is less and less the situation in many countries today. The point is not simply that our neighbors may come from different cultures and practice different religions. It is that the kind of complex intellectual formation that I have just said characterizes scholars such as Stalnaker, Bucar, and Clairmont is not unique to professional scholars of comparative ethics. Rather, it is arguably the case for more and more of our population. We live in a world in which many young people are not simply exposed to but grapple with materials from a variety of cultural backgrounds in the midst of their own most profound intellectual formation.

This claim risks being misunderstood as underestimating the depth of cultural and historical distances: I do not mean to say that we can all already understand everyone. Nonetheless, we have a variety of undergraduates whose first systematic reflection on virtue takes place in a course on early Chinese thought or medieval Islam. Even for the student who does not go on to become a scholar, this encounter may

---

[46] He qualifies this conception on 198, but one wishes that qualification played a more substantial role in the work's framing at the outset.

[47] See Clairmont, *Moral Struggle and Religious Ethics*, 209. For MacIntyre's discussion of second first languages, see MacIntyre, *Whose Justice? Which Rationality?* (Notre Dame, IN: University of Notre Dame Press, 1988), 370–88.

profoundly shape what become his or her "native," even intuitive, views on these matters. Again, this is not to claim that such a student should really be considered a Confucian. Nor is it to discount important elements of a broader contemporary intellectual and cultural context. It is simply to point out that those encounters not infrequently take place at crucial points in individuals' formation, such that they have a deep impact and are no longer adequately characterized as simply "other." Moreover, despite their impact on North Atlantic culture, students may not find Aristotle or Augustine less "other" than Xunzi or Buddhaghosa in such contexts.

The result is emphatically not that we are simply all cosmopolitans now. Rather, attending to these characteristics of the formation taking place in and around us should lead us to appreciate the complex particularity of individuals'—and sometimes groups'—ethical and intellectual identities. We are not dealing with unified cultural or religious wholes colliding with each other. Presenting "the modern (or postmodern) West" as a relatively unified or singular standpoint, rather than a complex plurality, becomes less and less tenable. Otherness is not thereby denied but rather fragmented and multiplied, though not radicalized.

I suspect that this feature of our context is in no small degree a result of the diversification of university curricula in recent decades. For instance, it may not be a coincidence that both Stalnaker and Schofer were undergraduates at Stanford University when, amidst heated debate, that institution replaced its Western Culture Program with Cultures, Ideas and Values, which sought to bring global diversity to its required curriculum. Such historical claims, however, are beyond the scope of the present inquiry.

No less important is the impact of post-1965 immigration to the United States. As Diana Eck has argued in relation to religion in particular, the result has been increasing cultural diversification in our universities as well as our society more broadly.[48] The consequences include not only increasing numbers of scholars of comparison whose family backgrounds mean they have a particularly complex relationship to "the Western tradition." They also entail

---

[48] Diana L. Eck, *A New Religious America: How a "Christian Country" Has Now Become the World's Most Religiously Diverse Nation* (San Francisco: HarperSanFrancisco, 2001). I thank Grace Kao for highlighting the significance of this historical development.

that even those of us whose families were not part of this immigration may have been deeply shaped by contacts with people whose families were. Notions of "the modern West" have thereby become ever more complex.

Stalnaker highlights increasing diversity as well as increasing communication and interactions with people in other parts of the world as an important rationale for comparison itself.[49] My point, however, is different: it is that such encounters are not simply all around us but already within us. If that is the case, then it is all that much clearer that there are no encounters that are not comparative in the relevant sense. Although for most people in and around North Atlantic universities today there are vast quantitative differences between the challenges involved in engaging the work of Kant and that of Xunzi, these differences cannot be adequately understood in terms of one being a modern Westerner (and thus one of "us") and the other not.

All of these points suggest that the methodological challenges inherent in comparative studies are not as unique as often supposed. To the contrary, the task of comparison places in relief issues that are no less involved in studies of a single figure, whether or not that figure is from a very different time and place than the interpreter. To be sure, the practical challenges are typically immensely greater: learning about two distinct historical contexts, two sets of languages, and so forth. But the methodological challenges that comparative studies make explicit are implicit in all of our attempts to interpret others, even those close to us.

A UNIQUE VALUE OF COMPARISON?

In making the case that central fruits of recent theorization of comparison are no less relevant to studies that are not explicitly comparative, the above discussion highlights the value of recent work that has been labeled "comparative religious ethics." Nonetheless, this claim leaves open the question whether comparative religious ethics should be its own subfield. Even if the methodology of explicitly comparative studies is not qualitatively different from that of studies focused on

---

[49] Stalnaker, *Overcoming Our Evil*, 2–3.

one object (whether a text, thinker, or subject of an ethnography), there might be other rationales to designate "CRE" as a distinct subfield. The two most obvious candidates for such justification would seem to be (1) that explicitly comparative studies as such have a unique value that cannot be served by other kinds of studies and (2) that in the present circumstances there are strategic reasons for a distinct label such as CRE: only in this way will these important works receive the attention they deserve. I focus on the first of these candidates and take up the second briefly at the end.

In asking about a unique value to (explicitly) comparative studies, the question is not whether there is value in particular studies that are comparative—I argue that there often is—but whether comparative studies as such have such a distinctive value that they merit their own subfield. Do explicitly comparative studies, by virtue of their double-barreled approach, offer a type of contribution unattainable by other means? Comparativists have devoted significant energy to arguments justifying why we should compare, and these arguments often appear to claim that there is something special in comparison, that "in comparison a magic dwells," to borrow Jonathan Z. Smith's characterization of conceptions of comparison that he is critiquing.[50] If explicitly comparative studies as such offer something that single-subject studies cannot, then perhaps they merit a distinct subfield even if they do not involve a fundamentally distinct method.

In responding to this nexus of issues, I want to argue both that comparative studies can be extraordinarily valuable and that this value is not of a sort that justifies comparative religious ethics as a distinct subfield. Most fundamentally, comparative studies can be remarkably effective in helping us to understand both of the figures, as well as ourselves, in ways that we would not have had we not engaged in the comparison. Bringing well-chosen figures (or texts or groups) together may lead us to notice assumptions that would have easily gone unnoticed, offer resources to strengthen rational reconstructions, and make us more self-conscious about our own presuppositions. The juxtapositions draw our attention to facets of each thinker that we might not have otherwise noticed. This aspect of the value of comparison is fundamentally heuristic, and the value of any given comparison must be judged heuristically.

---

[50] Jonathan Z. Smith, "In Comparison a Magic Dwells," in *Imagining Religion: From Babylon to Jonestown* (Chicago: University of Chicago Press, 1982), 19–35.

This criterion entails, I would argue, that challenges regarding why to compare a particular set of figures (Xunzi and Augustine, for instance) are often misguided. They frequently presuppose that a comparison must be motivated by a unique appropriateness of that comparison. But there is no reason to accept this presupposition. To say that it is worthwhile to compare Xunzi and Augustine on spiritual exercises is not to say that it would not be valuable to compare Xunzi and Ignatius of Loyola or Augustine and Ignatius of Loyola on spiritual exercises—just as to say that it is worth studying Luther's influence on Kant is not to say that it would not be valuable to study Rousseau's influence on Kant. In each case, the significance of the study must be judged according to how much it illuminates the relevant figures. Although preliminary judgments on such matters are what motivate scholars to invest themselves in carrying out such studies in the first place, the ultimate judgment can only be made on the basis of the fruits of the study. Thus, when discussing "Why Xunzi and Augustine?" in his opening chapter, Stalnaker writes, "[a]t this point, the founding judgment of this study that both Xunzi and Augustine have particularly profound vocabularies for overcoming human evil can only serve as a promissory note, to be cashed in detailed analyses of their prescriptions."[51] The same goes not only for other similar comparisons but also for studies of Rousseau's influence on Kant (a study that would not typically be considered an instance of CRE). Appropriately, much of the debate over the value of particular scholarly work concerns just how much its particular angle of inquiry—whether or not comparative—illuminates a particular figure or question. We judge all such studies for their capacity to enable us to see, understand, and judge aspects of figures that would have otherwise gone unnoticed or inadequately appreciated.[52]

These points suggest that explicitly comparative studies, when done well, constitute important scholarly contributions. My goal is in no sense to downplay their significance. They advance our ability to understand and judge texts, thinkers, and movements. In doing so,

---

[51] Stalnaker, *Overcoming Our Evil*, 20.

[52] On the heuristic value of comparison, see also Thomas A. Lewis, "Frames of Comparison: Anthropology and Inheriting Traditional Practices," *Journal of Religious Ethics* 33, no. 2 (2005): 225–53. For a compelling account of method in comparison as ultimately coming down to "a fine-grained comparison of competing interpretations based on the back and forth between close reading and history" rather than "a grand comparative enterprise," see Davis, *Believing and Acting*, 172.

however, they contribute to the same broad goals as scholarship by figures such as Jean Porter and Jennifer Herdt, neither of whom is explicitly comparative in her methodology. The point is not that Stalnaker should or would have gained the same insights about Augustine had he not been comparing him with Xunzi. I doubt he would have. Even though Stalnaker's specific study makes a unique contribution, however, there is no unique contribution attached to comparison as such. Moreover, the goods pursued and attained are of the same sort, and the fruitfulness of a particular comparison is to be judged by the same, heuristic criteria we use to judge whether Hegel's early writings hold the key to interpreting his mature thought; such criteria are not unique to explicitly comparative projects. Despite the great value of particular comparative studies, this value does not call for a distinct subfield.

Some scholars, however, offer defenses of comparison that could be read as suggesting a unique value that could not be served, even in principle, by studies that are not explicitly comparative. Such claims merit closer scrutiny. A number of comparativists highlight the value of learning about cultures other than our own. Undoubtedly, there is much value in doing so, particularly in a world as interconnected as our own (however fuzzy the lines are). Learning about others has tremendous power to make us appreciate and respect others more, as well as to engage in meaningful arguments—not just shouting matches—when we disagree on points of common concern. The benefit moves in both directions: comparisons frequently enable us to see ourselves in new ways, placing our own unconscious assumptions in relief. As Stalnaker and others stress, these benefits are all that much more important when our next-door neighbors are deeply shaped by materials that we would initially encounter as other. Stalnaker's "global neighborliness" is important not only for negotiating an increasingly interconnected globe but also for making one's way through one's own neighborhood.[53]

As important as these ends are, however, they are not unique to explicitly comparative projects. In fact, these are rationales for learning about others, not for comparative projects as such. Of course, these ends do require learning about communities other than one's own, but many kinds of studies of other communities and figures do this, whether or not they are explicitly comparative. The point comes out well when one notices the commonalities between the rationales offered by Stalnaker, Clairmont, and Bucar, on one hand, and Richard Miller, on the other. In "On Making a Cultural Turn in Religious Ethics," Miller draws extensively on the anthropologists James Clifford, Michael Fischer, and George Marcus to argue for the value of studying other cultures as a means to learning about oneself.[54] Such studies both relativize much that we take for granted and make us aware of alternative ways of conceiving basic features of our own culture. Miller notes that "their work provides a rationale for comparative inquiry"; but it is no less apparent that such benefits can be gained by reflective, self-conscious studies that focus on the study of one cultural context (rather than two or more).

More significantly, the extent to which *this* goal of comparison is served depends not on whether two or more figures are central objects of comparison but on how explicitly the audience's own assumptions (however complex they may be) are taken up and made explicit in the inquiry. Schofer's explicit elaboration of his own categories in terms of influential recent theory arguably serves this goal more effectively than a focus on two ancient figures (in the absence of explicit reflection on the relation to our own intellectual repertoires).[55] Further, insofar as our goal is to understand our neighbors today, studies of our contemporaries may well be more valuable than studies of ancient figures, even influential ones, whether from the West or the East. Crucially, though, my point is not that studying ancient figures is unimportant but that the rationales sometimes offered for comparison may not be as applicable to some of the most important comparative studies (such as Yearley's and Stalnaker's) as they are to studies of contemporary communities—such as Saba Mahmood's examination of women's piety movements in Cairo in the 1990s—that are not comparative in this sense.[56] The conclusion, it seems to me, is that we need to be more

[54] Richard B. Miller, "On Making a Cultural Turn in Religious Ethics," *Journal of Religious Ethics* 33, no. 3 (2005): 413–15. His excellent account of their limits is no less important.

[55] See Schofer, *Making of a Sage*, "Self, Subject, and Chosen Subjection," and *Confronting Vulnerability.*

[56] Saba Mahmood, *Politics of Piety: The Islamic Revival and the Feminist Subject* (Princeton: Princeton University Press, 2005). Thus, I share Lee's view that Stalnaker's work may contribute less to our negotiation of today's pluralistic societies than Stalnaker suggests; Lee, "Rhetoric of Context," 575. Nonetheless, there is still much to value in Stalnaker's comparison.

pluralistic about the ends pursued by various studies as well as the kinds of studies that can support these ends. Viewed from another angle, my point is not that such figures are not worth studying. It is that the same kinds of reasons that make them worth studying comparatively also make them worth studying "non-comparatively." Comparison does not have a unique justification here. Stalnaker and others make an important case for the value of learning about others, but it is not a case for comparison as such.

In her discussion of Iranian Shi'i and U.S. Catholic women, Bucar makes a more specific point that merits consideration. In addition to the more general arguments for the value of comparison discussed above, she argues that, in light of the contemporary global political situation, there is particular value in better understanding groups such as the Iranian women she is studying: "The ability to remain open to multiple perspectives is especially important given recent geopolitical events when the Unites States seems poised for war with Iran. Considering the Shi'i perspective alongside one that is more prominent in U.S. politics will help counter impressions of Iran as backward, irrational, or evil."[57] I do not doubt Bucar's general point here, and I think it is an important part of the justification for this particular comparison. But I question whether the end is uniquely well served by double-barreled comparative studies. Is the goal necessarily more directly served by a study of Iranian Shi'i and U.S. Catholic women than studies comparable to Mahmood's study of women's piety movements in Cairo or John Kelsay's investigation of the background of contemporary Islamic arguments about just war?[58] (Of course, both of these works can be understood as comparative, but precisely as we expand the category of "comparative" the line between comparative religious ethics and the rest of religious ethics begins—helpfully—to fade; this is my point.)

This point may come out more clearly if we imagine potential responses to Bucar's project by certain kinds of feminists. It is not difficult to imagine a response quite different from that which Bucar seems to anticipate. The comparison itself might prompt some to retort, "You see, even those seemingly progressive Catholic women are no better than the Iranian Shi'i women. Even though I share Frances Kissling's interest in challenging the Vatican's teaching on

---

[57] Bucar, *Creative Conformity*, xxiii.
[58] Mahmood, *Politics of Piety*, and Kelsay, "Arguing the Just War."

abortion, this work brings out the extent to which even she is still unable to think independently of that tradition." Of course, much could be said to counter such a reaction. But the potential response brings out something crucial. The work's ability to shift an audience member's thinking, to make him or her more open to the Iranian women's perspectives, likely depends less on the comparison between them and U.S. Catholic women than on the extent to which that audience member's own position (which may or may not share a great deal with these U.S. Catholic women) is engaged. It is not the double-barreledness of the comparison that matters for this goal. It is the extent to which particular readers are spoken to, either through expressing a group's views in categories familiar to the reader or through expanding or transforming the categories with which the reader initially approached the study. For some of Bucar's readers— such as (but not limited to) many U.S. Catholic women—that will be accomplished by explicitly including U.S. Catholic women as one arm of a comparison. Others, however, might benefit (with respect to the specific goal of "counter[ing] impressions of Iran as backward, irrational, or evil") more from a treatment closer to the works of Schofer or Mahmood, who explicitly frame their studies in relation to the theoretical categories that many of their (academic) readers likely take for granted.

Like Bucar, Stalnaker also makes a more specific point about the value of studying ethical formation comparatively. Such studies are particularly valuable for societies, such as ours, that are "culturally and religiously complex and disintegrated."[59] He suggests that comparative studies such as his provide "a way to move beyond the simplistic tradition/modernity dichotomy" that has characterized influential recent discussions in religious ethics, particularly those influenced by Alasdair MacIntyre and Stanley Hauerwas.[60] Viewing spiritual exercises as something other than the unique property of isolated traditions may enable us to think through how models of ethical cultivation might be retrieved in a complex situation such as our own. Doing so, for instance, may help us to see how certain elements of a thinker's picture might be retrieved independently of the social context in which they originally developed. Stalnaker's point is thought provoking, and it counts toward the fruitfulness of

---

[59] Stalnaker, *Overcoming Our Evil*, 4.   [60] Stalnaker, *Overcoming Our Evil*, 4.

his comparison. Moreover, this particular benefit appears to derive specifically from the comparative aspect of the project. While Stalnaker frames this point in terms of his specific theme (spiritual exercises), one might offer a parallel rationale for other comparative studies: the comparison places in relief the question of what elements of an intellectual position are able to stand independently of the historical context, as well as—in some cases—certain metaphysical claims, in which they were originally embedded. This is a potentially significant contribution, and Stalnaker makes a convincing case that comparative studies can be particularly well suited for such a project. Even here, however, it is not clear that explicitly comparative studies are unique in pursuing or achieving this goal. To the contrary, much scholarship on historical figures takes up the question of "what is living and what is dead" in a thinker and asks how dependent a thinker's ethical views are on her or his metaphysical commitments.[61] As important as the goal is and as valuable as comparative studies can be in pursuing it, neither the goal nor its effective pursuit distinguish explicitly comparative studies.

If CRE as a distinct subfield is justified neither by a distinct method nor a distinct goal, we might still ask whether practical or strategic considerations about highlighting the work justify—at least at present—talking about it as its own subfield. After all, the discussion above highlights how important recent comparative studies have been; I in no sense want to render them less visible. While a distinct rubric may add visibility in some sense—by justifying conferences, special issues of journals, and so forth—my concern is that the space thereby created and preserved for explicitly comparative work is a marginal one. Excellent conversations are fostered and much good work is done. Nonetheless, the majority of scholars of religious ethics remain outside these circles and—precisely because they understand CRE as something discrete and separate from what they do—appear justified in largely ignoring this body of work. Its broad and deep significance for religious ethics as a whole thereby goes largely unappreciated.

---

[61] I borrow the phrase from Benedetto Croce, *What Is Living and What Is Dead of the Philosophy of Hegel*, trans. Douglas Ainslie (London: Macmillan, 1915). Allen Wood, in *Hegel's Ethical Thought* (Cambridge: Cambridge University Press, 1990), offers a good example of someone who seeks to retrieve a figure's ethical thought independently of any larger metaphysical picture that figure may offer.

THE RESULTING VISION

Considering together (1) the broader implications of reflection on methodology in comparative studies and (2) the way that a variety of kinds of studies can pursue the benefits touted by comparative religious ethics suggests something important about the way we ought to conceptualize religious ethics as a whole. The methodological challenges highlighted by those theorizing comparison are not unique to comparison but are intrinsic to any interpretive endeavor—even if they are more obvious and quantitatively greater in cases of explicit comparison. These challenges cannot be avoided by efforts to eschew comparison in favor of understanding others "on their own terms." At the same time, advocates of comparison (among others, of course) make a strong case for studying people from contexts very different from our own, though the case that studies must themselves have two or more objects of comparison in order to pursue the relevant goal is much weaker.

Rather than conceiving of comparative religious ethics as a distinct subfield, then, I propose we conceive of religious ethics as a whole in terms of a conversation that brings together studies focused on a wide range of texts, thinkers, and groups. The topics or issues will be those of "ethics," but the meaning of this concept—along with others that frame the inquiries and conversation—will be open to ongoing transformation. Scholars with expertise in particular areas—such as contemporary Protestant thought, early Taoism, medieval Islamic thought, and so forth—will contribute to a common conversation about the topics at hand—such as the nature of ethical obligation itself, accounts of human flourishing, habituation, and more specific topics such as issues in just war theory. To describe this as a common conversation is not to say that we are all already in a position to understand each other well; that is an ongoing and constantly evolving task. Rather, it is simply to say that we are dealing with a single, larger but variegated field of inquiry, not several different fields. On some topics (perhaps views of sexual behavior), we may find that there is little ground for meaningful exchange without turning to additional aspects of a thinker's view. My proposal does not assume that on any given topic any group can sit down and immediately have productive exchanges. A number of scholars have argued for the fruitfulness of anthropology or conceptions of the self as a locus for such conversations, but the more general point is to explore empirically where conversations can gain traction.[62]

Admittedly, important aspects of the vocabulary in which the conversation is conducted will initially derive from Western traditions of inquiry, and Christianity in particular. This predominance derives from the social and historical location of much contemporary work in religious ethics as well as the distribution of areas of specialization within religious ethics. It is vital to acknowledge this reality as well as to distinguish the kinds of privilege this does and does not confer. It does mean that more of the conversation will focus directly on topics and materials emerging from this history and that the most widely circulating questions, concepts, and categories will, at least at present, have emerged from this tradition. It does not, however, entail that these latter should not be challenged or should remain dominant in the field; they do not have any special authority. Nor does it entail that scholars of Christian materials have less responsibility to engage scholars of materials from other traditions than the other way around. The concepts should be revised as well as added to over the course of the inquiries—just as happens in most real conversations over time.

While even this degree of privilege can be seen as a downside of my vision, the implication of the above discussion about the import of our own concepts and categories in the analysis is that *this* kind of privilege is inevitable. We do not understand and interpret from an Archimedean standpoint but from where we already stand. And insofar as we are talking about conversations in the North Atlantic academy, we are dealing with more people whose standpoints are largely shaped by these Western materials—the demographic and curricular shifts discussed above notwithstanding. The closest thing to an alternative would be to attempt to ignore others and to work in

---

[62] See Thomas A. Lewis et al., "Anthropos and Ethics: Categories of Inquiry and Procedures of Comparison," *Journal of Religious Ethics* 33, no. 2 (2005): 177–85; Mark A. Berkson, "Conceptions of Self/No-Self and Modes of Connection: Comparative Soteriological Structures in Classical Chinese Thought," *Journal of Religious Ethics* 33, no. 2 (2005): 293–331; Lewis, "Frames of Comparison"; Schofer, "Self, Subject, and Chosen Subjection"; Aaron Stalnaker, "Comparative Religious Ethics and the Problem of 'Human Nature,'" *Journal of Religious Ethics* 33, no. 2 (2005): 187–224, as well as Elizabeth M. Bucar, Grace Y. Kao, and Irene Oh, "Sexing Comparative Ethics: Bringing Forth Feminist and Gendered Perspectives," *Journal of Religious Ethics* 38, no. 4 (2010): 654–9.

silos as much as possible, though even that is less of an alternative than it might initially appear. Instead, I advocate greater reflexivity and self-consciousness about the concepts we bring to bear as well as an explicit willingness to revise these through encounters with others. Though we will never be entirely aware of our presuppositions, we are better off continuing to ferret them out than hoping they do not exist.

This arguably modest proposal contrasts with John Kelsay's recent argument that we ought to resume something like the comparative project proposed by David Little and Sumner Twiss in their *Comparative Religious Ethics*.[63] In his judgment, the abandonment of Little and Twiss's efforts to develop a broad classificatory scheme to frame comparative religious ethics as a discipline has been a loss. Without such a framework, he argues, it will be impossible for CRE to advance as a discipline. Notably, Kelsay and I largely agree regarding which developments have dominated CRE in the last two decades and agree that these works threaten a notion of CRE as a distinct discipline. These judgments lead Kelsay to argue for resuming Little and Twiss's broad agenda. By contrast, I hold that the arguments—developed by Stout as well as many contributors to Lovin and Reynolds' *Cosmogony and Ethical Order*—that led the field away from Little and Twiss's paradigm are largely sound. It is the notion of CRE as a distinct discipline—not these arguments—that must be abandoned. In order to argue convincingly for the alternative, Kelsay needs to offer a far more robust critique of the family of criticisms of Little and Twiss's strategy than he has to date. At the same time, Kelsay's worries that the alternative results in little more than a series of "edifying discourses" is overstated.[64] Comparative religious ethics—or religious ethics more generally—need not be a discipline in Kelsay's sense to make substantive contributions to the understanding and critical assessment of ethical views and practices.[65]

For some, my proposal will not appear novel; it will describe what religious ethics already is. I want to emphasize two points however: first, religious ethics so conceived should be increasingly self-conscious about the central concepts and categories through which inquiry is

---

[63] John Kelsay, "The Present State."

[64] Kelsay, "The Present State," 584, 591.

[65] Again, Davis provides a powerful account of a more modest conception of comparison; see *Believing and Acting*, especially 172.

pursued. These should not simply be adopted unconsciously and uncritically from the material under examination, whether this be from cultural contexts near or far. Second, scholars of religious ethics should be open to learning both from and about ethics research on areas other than their own specialties (e.g., rabbinic ethics, Catholic moral theology, Japanese Buddhism, etc.). That does not mean being an expert in everything, but it may mean—for example—taking seriously scholarship on accounts of self-formation coming from rabbinic thought even though one is working principally on materials from a very different context. Even without being an expert in that field or in a position to conduct original research in that area—such as possessing the necessary languages—engagement with scholarship on that material may do much to place one's own presuppositions in relief. And its chances of doing so are much greater to the extent that that scholarship is self-conscious and explicit about the concepts that it deploys and their relationships to both the source materials and other contemporary scholarship.

One aspect of my point here can be expressed in terms of appreciating the extent to which all interpretation is comparative. It is easy to see such a statement as trivializing comparison. Insofar as I seek to challenge the notion of comparative religious ethics as a distinct subfield, I am in some sense guilty as charged. Yet the accusation easily conceals what can and should be learned from recognizing the crucial and non-self-evident role that our concepts play in any act of understanding. Moreover, this role of concepts is all that much more important to have in mind when we are studying materials whose operating concepts are significantly different from our own. For this reason, the point is far from trivial.

In conceptualizing religious ethics as a whole in this manner, my proposal involves taking Stalnaker's, Bucar's, and others' emphasis on learning about others a step further. First, my proposal expands the ways that we conceive of our own context, so that concepts, ideas, and arguments that come from other times and places are important for and constitutive of the discourse of religious ethics as a whole (not simply of some subfield, CRE). At the same time, I seek to support a wide range of work on ethical thought and practices from other contexts as integral to religious ethics—in a manner that enriches our resources for engaging with other cultures and peoples. Moreover, the proposal provides ways of thinking about and making more integral to religious ethics the contributions of historical and ethnographic scholarship, such as that championed by Bucar, Davis, Miller, and Schofer.[66]

A further implication of the points at issue here merits special notice. Recognizing (1) the extent to which virtually all scholars of religion today are already shaped by encounters (of multiple sorts) with a number of different intellectual and religious heritages *as well as* (2) the fact that an earlier figure in the scholar's "own tradition" may use particular concepts very differently than the scholar did at the beginning of the investigation entails that investigating "one's own tradition" is no excuse for foregoing careful scrutiny of the categories of analysis. Contemporary scholars who self-identify as Christians, for instance, should not assume that the hermeneutical challenges involved in interpreting Augustine are qualitatively different from those involved in studying Xunzi or late antique rabbis. Of course, Augustine's conceptualization of basic categories has historically influenced those of inheritors of contemporary Western culture, but claims to a common "tradition" should not obscure the distance of that influence.[67] Concretely, such claims do not obviate the need for the hard work of careful interpretation and critical inquiry. Moreover, the extent of influence should be part of the object of investigation, not its presupposition. To do otherwise is to fail to hold the academic study of religion to the same standards as other disciplines in the academy today. To make such a claim is in no way to invalidate the kind of investigation of one's own intellectual heritage pursued in works such as Charles Taylor's *Sources of the Self: The Making of the Modern Identity*, J. B. Schneewind's *The Invention of Autonomy: A History of Modern Moral Philosophy*, or Jennifer Herdt's *Putting on Virtue: The Legacy of the Splendid Vices.*[68] To the contrary, it is integral to such work. Nor is it to downplay our own particular situatedness in multiple, complex communities. It is,

---

[66] See Bucar, "Methodological Invention"; Davis, "Two Neglected Classics" and *Believing and Acting*; Miller, "Making a Cultural Turn"; and Schofer, "Embodiment and Virtue." See also Thomas A. Lewis, "Ethnography, Anthropology, and Comparative Religious Ethics: Or Ethnography and the Comparative Religious Ethics Local," *Journal of Religious Ethics* 38, no. 3 (2010): 395–403.

[67] Schofer, *Confronting Vulnerability*, 6–9, is very helpful on these points.

[68] Charles Taylor, *Sources of the Self: The Making of the Modern Identity* (Cambridge: Harvard University Press, 1989); J. B. Schneewind, *The Invention of Autonomy: A History of Modern Moral Philosophy* (Cambridge: Cambridge University Press, 1998); and Jennifer A. Herdt, *Putting on Virtue: The Legacy of the Splendid Vices* (Chicago: University of Chicago Press, 2008).

however, to challenge the notion that such situatedness can be adequately captured by categories such as "Thomistic Catholic," "modern Jew," or "evangelical Christian"—however indispensable such categories may be for other purposes. In other words, as important as it might be for someone to identify as or be identified as an Augustinian, it is not self-evident what this means; and the project of unpacking what it means to particular individuals or in particular contexts is precisely the task of interpretation and critical judgment. Appeals to authority, tradition, or canon cannot provide an intellectually respectable end-run around such work.

While my proposal might be seen as a threat to comparative inquiry, it is in another sense a proposal for comparative religious ethics to expand its reach. Given the challenges of becoming trained to do excellent scholarship on materials from two distinct historical, intellectual, and linguistic contexts, if we conceive of comparative religious ethics exclusively in terms of double-barreled studies such as those of Yearley, Stalnaker, Bucar, and Clairmont, then comparative religious ethics will remain marginal and sparsely populated. If we conceive of it as simultaneously taking on the "major" religions of the world, it will be even more marginal and most often more superficial. Consequently, to conceive of comparative religious ethics in these forms risks that the most significant insights yielded from reflection on methods of comparison will themselves be consigned to this small realm. By contrast, I argue for the broader significance of these fruits in bringing greater self-consciousness to the field of religious ethics as a whole. And nothing I have said should be understood to imply that classically comparative studies should be discouraged: to say that the value of a particular study should be judged vis-à-vis the same kinds of goals pursued by other forms of scholarship—rather than some *sui generis* goal—renders it neither more nor less intrinsically valuable than these other forms. The proof of the pudding is in the tasting, not in being a different kind.

Happily, significant recent work associated with comparative religious ethics seems to be moving in this direction. Scott Davis has championed Herbert Fingarette's *Confucius: The Secular as Sacred* (1972) as a "neglected classic of comparative ethics."[69] Fingarette's book focuses principally on Confucius's *Analects* but seeks to locate

---

[69] Davis, "Two Neglected Classics."

Confucius's contribution in relation to discussions in contemporary Western philosophy, thereby bringing his thought into a broader conversation on ethics. Similarly, Maria Heim's review essay on three recent works in Buddhist ethics explicitly connects these to larger discussions of moral anthropology and articulates the way these studies may contribute to religious ethics beyond Buddhist ethics.[70] And Jonathan Schofer's treatment of Mark Csikszentmihalyi's *Material Virtue: Ethics and the Body in Early China,* Edward Slingerland's *Effortless Action: Wu-wei as a Conceptual Metaphor and Spiritual Ideal in Early China,* Saba Mahmood's *Politics of Piety,* and Anna Gade's *Perfection Makes Practice: Learning, Emotion, and the Recited Qur'an in Indonesia*—as well as his own work on rabbinic materials—brings scholarship on these materials (which may not be explicitly comparative in itself) into a more inclusive religious ethics discourse. The same can be said of many of the contributions to the recent edited volume, *Religious Ethics in a Time of Globalism.*[71] While important double-barreled comparative studies (such as those of Bucar and Clairmont) continue to appear—and should continue to do so—this literature suggests that scholarship engaged with reflecting on comparison is moving toward situating itself within religious ethics more broadly. The line between "comparative religious ethics" and religious ethics more generally is becoming even blurrier than before.

While works such as these represent an important step in the right direction, another kind of progress lags behind. The works just mentioned all deal with non-Christian materials. Scholars working on such materials are generally expected to do much more to make these materials comprehensible to a broader audience. They must explicitly interrogate the basic categories and concepts of the analysis. Some degree of this may be inevitable; moreover, my own proposal assumes that the discourse of religious ethics will, at least for the near future, be structured largely by vocabulary emerging from Western intellectual traditions, and these will necessarily share more with Christianity than many other religions. Nonetheless, that point should not serve as an excuse to allow treatments of Christian materials—whether ancient

[70] Maria Heim, "Buddhist Ethics: A Review Essay," *Journal of Religious Ethics* 39, no. 3 (2011): 571–84, especially 574–6, 582–3.

[71] Elizabeth M. Bucar and Aaron Stalnaker, eds., *Religious Ethics in a Time of Globalism* (New York: Palgrave Macmillan, 2012).

or modern—to forgo the critical self-consciousness and scrutiny of categories in which scholars of other religions engage. Too often, doing so will not only leave crucial points unexamined; it will also project contemporary categories back onto materials from other times and places that may use the same or similar terms but with crucially different meanings. In other words, work on figures more familiar in the West should be held to the same high standards as work on materials that are less familiar in the Western academy today. Keeping in mind the fruits of reflection on the challenges of comparison will help to ensure that studies of earlier Western texts bring the same historical and linguistic sensitivity expected of scholarship on these other materials.

To hold that it is time to move beyond conceptions of comparative religious ethics as a distinct subfield is not to suggest the last three and a half decades of work in this area have not been fruitful. To the contrary, it is to say that what has been learned is no less relevant to religious ethics as a whole. In crucial respects, religious ethics as a whole should look more like what has been called comparative religious ethics. Building on the latter's fruits suggests a way of envisioning the field of religious ethics in a manner that is less Christian centered yet does not sacrifice a common conversation for the sake of inclusivity.

5

Against Religious Literacy

September 11 marks—among many other things—a watershed in the place of religion in the university. Previously, most presumed religion to be a relic of merely historical interest: in a secularized world, the study of its history might find a place in a few departments, but it was often deemed peripheral to the principal objects of research in the modern university. Early in the last decade, however, through 9/11 as well as the increasing visibility of the Christian right, religion announced—loudly—that reports of its death had been greatly exaggerated. Quickly, many scholars across the university came to see religion as worthy of study. Economists, political scientists, evolutionary biologists, and others, have endeavored to explain religion's endurance and power in the contemporary world. These efforts have energized the study of religion.

At the same time, scholars of religion have frequently lamented that this interest in religion among colleagues in other fields has rarely generated a corresponding level of interest in religious studies. Partly as a consequence, many of the resulting attempts to give religion more attention have shown profound methodological shortcomings—shortcomings that reveal the importance and urgency of recent methodological work in religious studies. Yet the methodological shortcomings exposed by religion's greater visibility as an object of academic inquiry are not unique to newcomers to studying religion. The transition to a more public stage has had its challenges for scholars of religion as well.

Reflecting on these challenges provides an ideal context to address broader issues about the structure of the study of religion. The issues at stake—concerning the way that notions of distinct religious traditions frequently structure the study of religion—concern not only matters for advanced seminars in theory and method but also the most urgent needs for the public understanding of religion. To develop this point, I use a critical examination of Stephen Prothero's influential championing of "religious literacy" as a springboard for considering the limits to structuring the study of religion, including departments of religious studies, in terms of the study of individual "religions" or "religious traditions," such as Christianity, Islam, and Buddhism. While I wholeheartedly support Prothero's contention that an informed public needs to understand religion better than it does, I argue that religious literacy as conceived by Prothero sets back, rather than advances, that goal. And the limitations of his focus on religious traditions are by no means unique to his project; rather, they continue to play an outsized role in structuring work in the field. Finally, I turn to two recent scholarly developments that move past the limitations of structuring the study of religion in terms of distinct religious traditions.

PROTHERO'S LIMITS

In response to the lack of knowledge about religion that seems to have left many of our politicians, planners, and pundits at a loss, one of the most prominent responses has been to call for "religious literacy." In *Religious Literacy: What Every American Needs to Know—And Doesn't* (first published 2007) and *God Is Not One: The Eight Rival Religions That Run the World—and Why Their Differences Matter* (2010), Stephen Prothero laments that despite being "one of the most religious countries in the world," we in the United States are simultaneously one of the least informed about religion.[1] The first of these books "begins with a paradox. . . . That paradox is this: Americans are both deeply religious and profoundly ignorant about religion."[2] The problem is not simply that the non-religious do not know about religion; even many of the most religious know remarkably little about their own religions:

---

[1] Stephen Prothero, *Religious Literacy: What Every American Needs to Know—And Doesn't* (San Francisco: HarperOne, 2008) and Stephen Prothero, *God Is Not One: The Eight Rival Religions That Run the World—and Why Their Differences Matter* (New York: HarperOne, 2010).

[2] Prothero, *Religious Literacy*, 1.

They [Americans] are Protestants who can't name the four Gospels, Catholics who can't name the seven sacraments, and Jews who can't name the five books of Moses. Atheists may be as rare in America as Jesus-loving politicians are in Europe, but here faith is almost entirely devoid of content. One of the more religious countries on earth is also a nation of religious illiterates.[3]

To be illiterate, then, is to fail to know what appear to be "basic facts" about various religions. Becoming somewhat more precise a few pages later, he writes, "religious literacy refers to the ability to understand and use the religious terms, symbols, images, beliefs, practices, scriptures, heroes, themes and stories that are employed in American public life."[4] Giving examples, he suggests that "Protestant literacy might refer to knowing the basic history of the Protestant Reformation, the core beliefs of the Christian creeds, and the basic symbols, heroes, and stories of the King James Bible, while Islamic literacy might refer to knowing basic Islamic history, the key practices of the Five Pillars of Islam, and the basic symbols, heroes, and stories of the Quran."[5] Prothero offers a 108-page "Dictionary of Religious Literacy" at the end of the book to provide some of this information. His next book, *God Is Not One*, seeks to offer religious literacy for "the eight rival traditions that run the world."

Prothero's rhetoric is powerful and has landed him spots on *The Daily Show* and *Colbert Report*. But even brief reflection on the purported paradox with which he begins *Religious Literacy* exposes a deep flaw in the project: if those who are deeply "religious" have so little "religious" knowledge, then we ought to wonder whether "religious" refers to the same thing in both halves of the sentence. *Pace* Prothero, what it means for most of these people to be religious is not centrally a matter of facts about scripture, for instance, as the rest of *Religious Literacy* effectively suggests it is or at least should be. This slippage between the "religious" of the first half of the sentence—the sense in which people in the United States are very religious—and "religious" in the second half of the sentence—pertaining to basic information about sets of texts, symbols, and stories—points to one of the most urgent tasks for religious studies. Scholars of religion need to do more than we have to provide conceptual and analytic resources

---

[3] Prothero, *Religious Literacy*, 1–2.
[4] Prothero *Religious Literacy*, 17.   [5] Prothero *Religious Literacy*, 15.

for understanding and explaining the kind of religiosity referred to in the first part of the sentence.

My point is not that knowledge about the Qur'an is irrelevant to understanding Muslims, for instance. But to think that it is the singular key is not just inadequate; it is profoundly misleading. Insofar as our goal is to understand the ways that religion moves elections and economies, for instance, Prothero's approach can leave us in a worse position than we were when we began.[6] For if we imagine that such knowledge constitutes the beginning of understanding the kinds of people Prothero wants to help us understand, we implicitly take for granted that religion is first and foremost a matter of subscribing to a set of claims contained in a body of texts that are taken to be uniquely authoritative. Even insofar as Prothero seeks to deemphasize doctrine and belief relative to other "dimensions of religion" in *God Is Not One*, he leaves intact the notion that the basic elements of understanding religious people consist in familiarity with scripture, the history of the religion's founding, the doctrinal issues at stake in its major ruptures, and so forth.

Precisely that understanding of religion leaves us dramatically unprepared to comprehend the myriad, complex ways that religion functions in people's lives. It hands us the wrong tools for the job but tells us these are what we need to get started. And when the tools do not work as promised, one obvious response is to suspect that there is something wrong with the object on which we are working. In this case, when people who understand themselves to be members of a tradition act in ways or hold beliefs that seem at odds with those texts, it becomes difficult to do more than throw up our hands and label them hypocritical, ignorant, or both.

Prothero offers a telling example in his treatment of Islam. Early in a subsection labeled "Jihad," Prothero reports a conversation he had with "a Muslim merchant I met in Jerusalem." The man "contend[ed] that jihad has nothing whatsoever to do with war because jihad is nothing more than the personal struggle to be good. 'Treating me with respect is jihad,' he said. 'Not ripping me off is jihad.' The Quran, he added, never even mentions war." Prothero ends his paragraph here, without further comment, then begins a new paragraph:

---

[6] Regarding these goals, see Prothero, *God Is Not One*, 8.

But the Quran does mention war, and it does so repeatedly. One Quranic passage commands Muslims to "fight," "slay," and "expel" in the course of just two sentences (2:190–1), while another says that fighting is "prescribed . . . though it be hateful to you" (2:216). Whether it is better for a religion's scriptures to largely ignore war (as in the Christian New Testament) or to carefully regulate war (as does the Quran) is an open question, but there is no debating the importance of the themes of fighting and killing in both the Quran and Islamic law.[7]

To be clear, Prothero is not arguing that Islam is more militaristic than Christianity or that Muslims are more violent than Christians (or atheists)—which is not to say there are not many reasons to challenge specifics of his treatment of Islam. What is revealing with regard to our purposes is the way that Prothero appeals to scripture to correct the Muslim with whom he is speaking. A charitable reading of Prothero might say that he does so simply to help us see how differently other Muslims understand the notion of jihad. Insofar as Prothero thereby highlights diversity within Islam, that is a good thing. In this respect, it is appropriately seen as one of the book's strengths. Yet he provides us with no resources for understanding these differences. If we want to understand religion's impact in the world—on politics, economics, etc.—then we need resources to think about how it is that one self-identified Muslim can contend that the "Quran . . . never even mentions war," while others presumably find the passages Prothero identifies to be prominent in their understanding of the Qur'an. Engaging that contrast should be absolutely central to the public understanding of religion, not a minor observation to be dropped and then left behind. Moreover, as Prothero acknowledges, the process of emphasizing some passages from canonical texts while largely ignoring others is in no sense unique to Islam.[8] To think that our engagement with such issues will be best divided and organized in terms of religious traditions lacks needed justification.

Prothero ends this section with a brief paragraph noting that despite "all the emphasis on jihad among Islamic extremists and Western neoconservatives," this is not one of Islam's central concepts. To the contrary, "the three keywords of the Islamic tradition are Allah, Muhammad, and the Quran. To see the world as Muslims

---

[7] Prothero, *God Is Not One*, 35.
[8] Prothero makes this point explicit with respect to Christianity; *God Is Not One*, 35.

see it, you need to look through these lenses."[9] As Prothero's previous page effectively illustrates, however, to "see the world as Muslims see it" is an impossibly fraught task, simply because different Muslims see the world in radically different ways. To direct our attention to what they have in common directs our attention away from the differences that are so important to the goals of understanding that are central to Prothero's project. These differences are no less significant than the differences across religious traditions. By talking about the way Muslims see the world as if this were a coherent or helpful category, we implicitly suggest that there is a genuine Muslim perspective. And, again, when we encounter individuals who claim to be Muslim but do not adhere to this account, we can do little but condemn them, whether for hypocrisy or ignorance.

Although one cannot deny that some religious people (like other people) are hypocritical, ignorant, or both, note what is lost when we are led too quickly to such explanations. If we manage to push past simply throwing up our hands and abandoning the inquiry out of frustration, we typically move next to trying to explain why these people are not acting as their religion tells them they ought to. And juxtaposing what their religion "really" tells them to do and what they are doing (perhaps even in the name of their religion) leads us toward explaining their behavior in ways that have nothing to do with religion. In other words, according to such accounts, the actual sources of their behavior are overruling the "religious" influences.

One set of objections to such a response would be that it too quickly abandons a hermeneutics of generosity or charity in favor of a hermeneutics of suspicion or critique of ideology: it too quickly rejects their self-interpretations in favor of an interpretation that explains their actions in terms they reject. There is much to this point. My general view is that we should work hard to make charitable interpretations work before abandoning these attempts in favor of explanations that portray texts or practices as systematically distorted. Yet the distinction between a hermeneutics of charity and of suspicion may be too rough to do the relevant work here, since a central issue concerns which aspects of a religious group's self-understanding we accept and which we reject—assuming that we will be doing some of both.

---

[9] Prothero, *God Is Not One*, 36.

In the present context, then, a more significant issue is that the above framing—in which people's religious influences are overruled or distorted by non-religious ones—presents religion as autonomous in relation to these other influences on or determinants of our behavior. These factors do not inform or mold religion itself but simply overrule it. Religion thus appears here once again as *sui generis* vis-à-vis other social and cultural factors. Note that we could make this point whether we conceive of these factors—religion, economic interests, and so forth—as external influences on agents or as constituting agency. In either case, if we conceive of religions in terms of largely fixed doctrines that are independent of other social and intellectual forces, attending to religion ultimately plays very little role in helping us understand what people do. We will find that we usually have to refer to factors other than what Prothero depicts as religions to explain crucial differences among Christians around the world, for instance. Appeals to religion will often then be interpreted as mere ideological cover for economic and political interests. Even though Prothero's project is aimed toward helping us to understand better religion's role in the contemporary world, it frames "religious literacy" in a way that tends to do the opposite.

The inadequacy of Prothero's approach comes out clearly in the closing pages of *God Is Not One*. Reiterating his point that people act not only on the basis of desires for money and power, he states that:

> people act every day on the basis of religious beliefs and behaviors that outsiders see as foolish or dangerous or worse. Allah tells them to blow themselves up or to give to the poor, so they do. Jesus tells them to bomb an abortion clinic or to build a Habitat for Humanity house, so they do. . . . To reckon with the world as it is, we need religious literacy. We need to know something about the basic beliefs and practices of the world's religions.[10]

Religious literacy is supposed to help us understand how religion shapes people's action in the world. Yet his own examples show why familiarity with the "basic beliefs and practices" of Islam or Christianity do not do the relevant work. If we want to understand religion's impact in the world, surely we care at least as much about the differences between those who understand Jesus to be telling them to bomb the abortion clinic and those who understand Jesus to be

---

[10] Prothero, *God Is Not One*, 337.

telling them to volunteer with Habitat for Humanity as we do about some abstract differences between Islam and Christianity. The former difference is crucial, and Prothero's "basic beliefs and practice of the world's religions" do little to help us comprehend it.

BROADER IMPLICATIONS FOR THE FIELD

In probing these limitations to the most influential account of religious literacy, my goal is to do more than simply criticize Prothero. As much as some scholars dismiss Prothero's religious literacy project as intellectually unserious, its problems are more reflective of broader tendencies in religious studies than many of us would like to admit. Prothero's structuring focus on religious traditions and very limited ability to explain differences within these traditions track more widespread ways of organizing the study of religion. Specifically, the limitations of his project prompt broader questions about the limits of structuring the study of religion in terms of distinct "religions" or "religious traditions." We see these implications most clearly by working through key elements of recent criticisms of the study of religion.

An important body of recent work on the history of the Western study of religion has argued that we ought to abandon the term religion.[11] To analyze this claim and its relevance to notions of religious traditions, it is valuable to distinguish between two levels of the argument: (1) the claim that "religion" is a constructed category rather than a natural kind simply out there to be discovered and (2) the claim that the category is intrinsically distorting, politically dangerous, and therefore ought to be abandoned.[12]

---

[11] Talal Asad, Tomoko Masuzawa, Timothy Fitzgerald, and Daniel Dubuisson each offer different versions of this kind of argument. See Talal Asad, *Genealogies of Religion: Discipline and Reasons of Power in Christianity and Islam* (Baltimore: Johns Hopkins University Press, 1993); Tomoko Masuzawa, *The Invention of World Religions, Or, How European Universalism Was Preserved in the Language of Pluralism* (Chicago: University of Chicago Press, 2005); Timothy Fitzgerald, *The Ideology of Religious Studies* (Oxford: Oxford University Press, 2000); Daniel Dubuisson, *The Western Construction of Religion: Myths, Knowledge, and Ideology*, trans. William Sayers (Baltimore: Johns Hopkins University Press, 2003).

[12] Kevin Schilbrack provides an excellent and more extended treatment of these issues. See Kevin Schilbrack, *Philosophy and the Study of Religions: A Manifesto* (Malden, MA: Wiley Blackwell, 2014), 85–111. My discussion of this point draws heavily on his.

The first claim is that religion is not a natural kind, that it has no essence that is out there, waiting to be properly identified. To the contrary, the term aggregates particular practices, beliefs, and/or experiences into wholes. These groupings are not dictated by the material itself but by a variety of interests on the part of those using the term. In this sense, it is constructed. As J. Z. Smith has famously put the point, "*there is no data for religion.* Religion is solely the creation of the scholar's study. It is created for the scholar's analytic purposes by his imaginative acts of comparison and generalization."[13] Smith's claim is not that the scholar fabricates data, but rather that the data does not self-identify as "religious" but is constituted as "religious" by virtue of the concepts, such as religion, that the scholar brings to bear. The category of religion is thus constructed by scholars (and others, as Kevin Schilbrack emphasizes) who use the term, rather than pre-existing as an entity out there to be discovered.[14]

Contrary to the claims of some, however, it does not follow from this claim alone that we should abandon the term religion. To claim that a particular concept is constructed, that it is not a natural kind, need not entail that it is false or nefarious. To the contrary, many of our concepts—from modern art, to liberalism, to subway—are constructed in just this sense and do important work. Construction need not entail illegitimacy or rejection.

The argument that we should abandon the category depends on the second level of argument identified above. Concerns about distortion typically incorporate and build upon claims that Western conceptions of religion inappropriately separate religion from other spheres of human activity, such as politics and economics, and/or posit genuine religion as fundamentally private or interior. Further, these conceptions of religion have been intimately interwoven with the exercise of power, even without our consciousness thereof. Talal Asad, for instance, suggests that the term is inextricable from histories of domination, particularly—though not exclusively—histories of Western colonialism:

> Defining what is religion is not merely an abstract intellectual exercise; it is not just what anthropologists or other scholars do. The act of

---

[13] Jonathan Z. Smith, *Imagining Religion: From Babylon to Jonestown* (Chicago: University of Chicago Press, 1982), xi.

[14] On the ways that Smith's phrasing is misleading, see Schilbrack *Philosophy and the Study of Religions*, 91.

defining (or redefining) religion is embedded in passionate dispute, it is connected with anxieties and satisfactions, it is affected by changing conceptions of knowledge and interest, and it is related to institutional disciplines. . . . When definitions of religion are produced, they endorse or reject certain uses of a vocabulary that have profound implications for the organization of social life and the possibilities of personal experience.[15]

At least in earlier work, Asad takes these concerns to require the abandonment of the term "religion." Its use is always "the historical product of discursive processes," such that we cannot simply use a particular version of the concept for heuristic purposes without entangling ourselves in processes of domination.[16]

Without denying the histories of domination in which the term religion has been implicated or our capacities to participate in those histories without awareness of doing so, however, we need to ask how unique these considerations are to the concept of religion. The same could be said for a host of other terms, including democracy, liberalism, domination, freedom, colonialism, and academia. This awareness should not lead us to stop using such terms; attempting to do so would leave us speechless. Rather, it demonstrates that we unavoidably make use of terms with complex, power-laden histories of which we are only partially aware. We cannot do without such concepts. What we need is greater self-consciousness and openness to revision in our use of the terms. If we reject the idea that "religion" ought to correspond to some essence that is out there to be discovered, we are freed to evaluate particular conceptions of religion for what they enable us to see. Concepts of religion can be appreciated as heuristic tools whose value should be judged relative to the particular inquiry at hand, not in terms of whether they capture what religion "really is." Perhaps more specifically, we need to ask whether particular definitions of the term are illuminating or obfuscating for the inquiry at hand.[17] This point will

---

[15] Talal Asad, "Thinking about Religion, Belief, and Politics," in *The Cambridge Companion to Religious Studies*, ed. Robert A. Orsi (Cambridge: Cambridge University Press, 2011), 39.

[16] Asad, *Genealogies of Religion*, 29.

[17] I thus side with J. Z. Smith, Kevin Schilbrack, and Bruce Lincoln in holding that an awareness of the constructedness of the category of religion need not lead us to abandon the term. See Smith, "Religion, Religions, Religious," in *Critical Terms for Religious Studies*, ed. Mark C. Taylor (Chicago: University of Chicago Press, 1998), 281; Schilbrack *Philosophy and the Study of Religions*, 85–111; and Bruce Lincoln,

prove particularly relevant in thinking about the role of notions of particular traditions in the study of religion.

As part of this attention to religion's construction, a number of scholars have focused on the construction of particular religious traditions—particularly Hinduism. Richard King and Tomoko Masuzawa, for instance, have each argued that various texts and practices were amalgamated into the entities Hinduism and Buddhism.[18] As Masuzawa puts this point with respect to Buddhism, prior to crucial developments in the nineteenth century, "neither European observers nor, for the most part, native 'practitioners' of those various devotional, contemplative, divinatory, funereal, and other ordinary and extraordinary cults that are now roundly called Buddhist had thought of those divergent rites and widely scattered institutions as constituting a single religion."[19] Masuzawa's point, of course, is not that those particular rites and so forth did not exist but that they were not thought of as collectively constituting a larger entity, the "world religion" Buddhism. King makes a similar claim regarding Buddhism and a comparable one for Hinduism.[20] European missionaries, colonial administrators, and scholars as well as South Asian elites synthesized a broad array of writings and practices into the religion of Hinduism. One facet of this process consisted in European scholars such as Anquetil-Duperron compiling a body of South Asian writings into a canon that could be seen as of a kind with Christian scripture.[21] Another aspect consisted of Indian scholars such as Vivekānanda forging and championing a "Hinduism" that could stand alongside other "great religions."[22]

Whether advanced by colonizers or indigenous elites, these scholars argue, notions such as "Hinduism" and "Buddhism" were constructed on the model of Protestantism, even if these were conceived as lesser instantiations (than Protestantism) of the broader type, religion. A body of literary texts were taken to constitute the

---

Holy Terrors: Thinking about Religion after September 11, 2nd edn. (Chicago: University of Chicago Press, 2006), especially 2–3.

[18] Richard King, *Orientalism and Religion: Postcolonial Theory, India and "the Mystic East"* (London: Routledge, 1999) and Masuzawa, *The Invention of World Religions*.

[19] Masuzawa, *The Invention of World Religions*, 122.

[20] King, *Orientalism and Religion*, especially 96–160.

[21] King, *Orientalism and Religion*, 119.

[22] King, *Orientalism and Religion*, 135–42.

authoritative scriptural bases of the religions, and there were frequent narratives of the tradition's decline into corruption and superstition (often mapping anti-Catholic polemics). While there is important room for debate on the specifics of these histories and whether some of these developments on the part of South Asian elites pre-dated colonial encounters, the larger point about the role of Protestantism or, in some cases, Christianity as a model for what have come to be described as the world religions of Hinduism and Buddhism remains powerful.

Reflecting on the limits of Prothero's project, however, reveals that the concerns about taking individual "religions" as the key units of analysis should run even deeper: the issue concerns not only those entities, such as Hinduism, that were formed through colonialism but also implicates the so-called tradition—whether conceived as Christianity or as Protestantism—that is treated as inappropriately projected. Even if the notion of Christianity, for instance, was not constructed through encounters with others or modeled on some other tradition, that does not in itself validate the notion for a given set of scholarly purposes. If scholars focused on the legacies of colonialism have drawn our attention to the political implications of the imposition of these categories on others, we should be no less attentive to the way that categories conceived and promoted by the group being studied involve their own forms of distortion. Even if the notion accurately reflects the self-understanding of many within "the Christian tradition," that tells us little about the concept's value for particular scholarly purposes. We need not settle on an answer to the question of the origins of the term Christianity to make the point that the collection of artifacts, practices, texts, and beliefs that are posited by this term as constituting a coherent whole do not automatically constitute a natural kind and should only be so grouped insofar as doing so is justified by the query at hand.[23] The key issue is not whether the notion of the tradition as a coherent entity was produced by external forces but whether grouping these materials together is illuminating for a particular project of research. We should

---

[23] William Arnal, for instance, has argued that the notion of Christianity emerged only in the second century CE and has been projected back into the first century. See William Arnal, "The Collection and Synthesis of 'Tradition' and the Second-Century Invention of Christianity," *Method and Theory in the Study of Religion* 23 (2011): 193–215, especially 194–5.

be no less concerned when a term that shapes scholarly enterprises derives from the self-legitimating practices of participants in a tradition—as when Christians justify their authority in terms of a connection to early Christian texts and communities—than when it results from the exercise of colonial power.

These considerations provide good reason not to consider religious traditions such as Hinduism, Buddhism, and Christianity to be self-evident. Rather, like religion itself, they are the creations of observers—not only scholars but also administrators, community authorities, and lay participants inside and outside the groups they identify. As in the case of the term religion, however, this recognition of the constructed character of these concepts need not in itself lead us to reject them. The arguments of J. Z. Smith, Bruce Lincoln, and Kevin Schilbrack with respect to the general term religion are helpful here. There may well be purposes for which these labels continue to be useful, assuming that we are self-conscious about that usage. That judgment can only be made with respect to particular purposes. For understanding religion's impact on the political choices people make today, for instance, I suspect they will be of limited utility. With regard to one of these traditions, Hinduism, Richard King argues against particular efforts to salvage the term "Hinduism," but even an argument such as his is best understood as holding that any particular use of the term will need to be carefully justified in light of the history of problematic assumptions behind the usage.[24] More generally, debates over the usage of such concepts are best negotiated with respect to particular topics of inquiry.

With this perspective in mind, we can say that the problem with notions of distinct but coherent religious traditions lies in the common practice of *not only* aggregating a series of religious beliefs, texts, and practices from diverse times and places, into individual "religions" *but also* using the resulting entities, such as Christianity, Islam, or Buddhism, as some of the basic units in terms of which religious studies structures our curricula, our graduate training, and our job descriptions. The crucial issue here is not the first of these steps in itself but the combination with the second. The organization of multiple phenomena into discrete groups is by no means inappropriate; it is a necessary aspect of understanding our world. Nor am

---

[24] King, *Orientalism and Religion*, 108–11.

I opposing the frequent value of organizing phenomena into categories such as Christian or Islamic.

My objection, rather, is to allowing these categorizations to do too much work in structuring the academic study of religion. Accepting these categories without critical scrutiny and awareness frequently involves taking over the self-understandings of members of particular religious groups—understandings that are themselves complicit in self-justifying claims to authority—and/or understandings produced by histories of domination, particularly colonialism. (Not coincidentally, it also tends to privilege knowledge that scholars of religion are likely to already have, since many of us have been trained in programs organized around these categories.) In either case, it will not do to take for granted their appropriateness for scholarly inquiries—or for increasing the public understanding of religion.

What I am advocating, then, is not abandoning altogether the role of concepts such as Christianity in the study of religion but rather using this organizing frame as one among others in our work. The point becomes clearer in relation to a concrete example. If we seek to understand the views of religion developed by the German thinker G. W. F. Hegel, who understood himself to be a Lutheran, it will be important to attend to his interaction with earlier Christian materials (even if many earlier Christian materials will be of negligible importance for understanding Hegel). We see this connection, to take one of many possible examples, in his treatment of Christian practices of communion. There Hegel develops his own view in relation to other classic Christian views and the rejection of Catholic accounts of transubstantiation.[25] Hegel's references here are explicit, and it is clear that knowledge of these other Christian discussions of communion will be vital for our interpretation of Hegel on these issues. Somewhat more subtly, Molly Farneth has recently argued that understanding Hegel's treatment of the concepts of confession and forgiveness in his *Phenomenology of Spirit* is crucially illuminated by seeing the way that Hegel's account is shaped by Luther's treatment of the practice of confession.[26] These references

---

[25] G. W. F. Hegel, *Lectures on the Philosophy of Religion*, trans. R. F. Brown, P. C. Hodgson, and J. M. Stewart, 3 vols. (Berkeley: University of California Press, 1984), 3:154–6. I have discussed these issues in Thomas A. Lewis, *Religion, Modernity, and Politics in Hegel* (Oxford: Oxford University Press, 2011), 221–2.

[26] Molly Farneth, "Hegel's Sacramental Politics: Confession, Forgiveness, and Absolute Spirit," *Journal of Religion* 95, no. 2 (2015): 183–97.

are more implicit than explicit in Hegel's text, however; and many interpreters of Hegel, particularly those in departments of philosophy, have missed them. Certainly, one important role that scholars of religion bring to interdisciplinary discussions on topics such as these is a familiarity with the relevant traditions and the ability to demonstrate where these aspects of a thinker's background are doing particular work.

But it is no less the case that understanding Hegel's views on religion requires engagement with Spinoza's impact on Hegel's intellectual world. Spinoza's not being Christian is irrelevant here; his work is far more important to understanding Hegel than that of many Christian figures. Hegel's religious views are also crucially shaped by his understanding of the social transformations being brought about by early modernity. An adequate account of Hegel's religious thought requires engaging with these factors no less than with earlier developments in "the Christian tradition." Only in this manner can we hope to understand the central role Hegel attributes to religion in providing social cohesion amidst rapid social, economic, and political transformations.

In examining Hegel's religious thought, there is no reason to award the category of Christianity a privileged place in framing our analysis. Earlier elements of Christianity will be important for the interpretation of his thought, and it will be meaningful in a variety of contexts to refer to him as Christian. We need not give up this category, but we do need to give up the assumption that categories such as these are the self-evident starting points or the dominant frames for our analysis of particular figures or groups.

At first glance, such points appear trivial and obvious. Few would advocate studying Hegel in a way that abstracts from Spinoza's influence or from his broader social context. Moreover, no one scholar can be equally versed in all aspects of this background, and one might well think that as scholars of religion we should focus particularly on the Christian elements of Hegel's background—that this should be our distinctive contribution to what should be interdisciplinary conversations, whether about a single figure such as Hegel, a movement such as liberation theology in Latin America, or prayer practices of women's piety groups in contemporary Egypt.

Crucially, however, to understand the role of the scholar of religion in these terms is to systematically leave her without adequate tools for grasping particular religious figures, groups, or materials. It attends to only one dimension of the background of the purported object of study (this figure, movement, or practice) and thereby leaves us without the resources needed to understand what it is that we purportedly study.

In addition to providing us with the resources to understand only one aspect of the relevant background, this manner of framing the study of religion also easily, if inadvertently, authorizes the self-justifications of religious groups that claim to stand in immediate relation to early forms of a tradition, as in various evangelical groups in the United States. Although knowledge of earlier instantiations of Christianity will be relevant to showing just how different such groups are from early Christian communities, for instance, it will not provide the resources to explain how particular communities have come to have the form they have. Such factors—including the broader social context and encounters with a variety of others—are systematically screened out. Moreover, even where discontinuities and variations are noted, an approach that seeks to understand contemporary Christian communities predominantly in relation to a "Christian tradition" subtly reinforces an ideal of continuity—a notion of faithfulness to original texts, founding figures, and early communities. Even where particular communities are found to be very different from the groups they claim as their authorities, structuring the study of religion in relation to these purported trajectories tends to legitimate the self-understandings of those within the tradition.

Beyond legitimating certain notions of continuity with origins, conceiving of religions as even roughly cohesive wholes in this manner easily obscures important differences within these traditions. This problem comes out clearly in a work such as Prothero's *God Is Not One*. For all Prothero's attention to differences within traditions, these are clearly subordinated to the differences between the eight different "rival religions" that are presented as the basic alternatives. Yet the point about the occlusion of differences within traditions still lingers in more sophisticated and subtle work in the field. To take one example, the Comparative Religious Ideas Project consisted in a substantial group of scholars of religion who met together in a series of conferences from 1995 to 1999 and produced three volumes.[27] The

[27] See Robert C. Neville, ed., *The Human Condition*, The Comparative Religious Ideas Project (Albany: State University of New York Press, 2001); Robert C. Neville,

scholars included six "specialists," with expertise "in different religions [and] with a strong commitment to historical specificity," as well as a number of "generalists," whose expertise was not defined principally in relation to a particular religious tradition even if they did possess more background in some traditions than others.[28] Their discussions and the resulting volumes focused on "the human condition, ultimate realities, and religious truth," substantial topics deemed well suited for comparative study. In the present context, what stands out is the presentation of the specialists in relation to the "traditions" about which they speak. Each of these scholars focuses on a particular period or even text of a given tradition, and the project is explicit about acknowledging differences and diversity within religious traditions. Despite making these qualifications, the project holds onto the rubrics of distinct religions to structure the project. They identify these traditions as "Buddhism, Chinese religion, Christianity, Hinduism, Islam, and Judaism." They defend this choice of traditions and aim to combine a focus on the particular texts or moments on which the individual specialists focus with broader claims about these six traditions. They define these religious traditions in terms of canonical texts and "motifs," arguing that despite the internal diversity, these traditions "form around and take their initial identify from these core texts and motifs in such a way that all subsequent developments in each tradition have to come to terms with them."[29] All Hindus have to come to terms with the Vedas; all Buddhists must somehow engage the Buddha's teachings and canonical accounts of his life; all Muslims relate to the Qur'an as authoritative; and so forth. Despite the acknowledged diversity within traditions, these project organizers take this conception of religious traditions to circumscribe sufficiently coherent entities to provide the basic units of comparison; and each of the three volumes proceeds accordingly.

There is much to be said for this way of conceiving of religious traditions. This is one reason I do not object to talk of religious traditions as such. I do not dispute that for certain purposes this

ed., *Religious Truth*, The Comparative Religious Ideas Project (Albany: State University of New York Press, 2001); Robert C. Neville, ed., *Ultimate Realities*, The Comparative Religious Ideas Project (Albany: State University of New York Press, 2001).

[28] Robert C. Neville, "Preface," in Neville, *The Human Condition*, xvi–xvii.
[29] Neville, "Preface," xx.

will be a useful way to conceive of certain traditions. Christians do seem to all take the New Testament as in some sense authoritative, for instance. I leave aside here the question of whether parallel claims hold for Hinduism or Chinese religions. Even in the case of Christianity, however, Christians disagree about the interpretation of this text, who is qualified to interpret it, the nature of its authority, the authority of other sources, and much else—as Neville and the other project organizers would readily concede. The concern, however, is not this diversity as such but the way that these differences bear on the topics at issue in the Comparative Religious Ideas Project. Crucially, the shared point of reference in canonical texts and the like does not generate a commonality of views of the human condition, ultimate realities, or religious truth. Christians who all take the New Testament as authoritative have held and continue to hold radically different views of the human condition. Consequently, the rationale provided for defining religious traditions as distinct but coherent entities does not justify their role in organizing a study of accounts of the human condition, ultimate realities, or comparable topics. There is a mismatch between the entities that are being taken as objects of comparison (religious traditions so conceived) and the topics with respect to which they are being compared. The category of religious traditions does not meaningfully organize responses to the questions about which they are asking. While the final pages of the preface generously take up a number of possible objections to their approach, this fundamental challenge is never fully engaged. Thus, even though claims about the unity of these traditions are explicitly and repeatedly qualified, the basic conception is retained and does much work in organizing the studies. It thereby reinscribes the notion that relevant differences within Christianity—or Islam, or Buddhism—are less significant than the commonalities. Without such an assumption, this manner of organizing the project lacks justification.

The Comparative Religious Ideas Project thus exemplifies an important point in our examination of the role of the notion of religious traditions in the study of religion. The problem is not the notion as such. The problem arises when the categories are asked to do work for which they are not suited, as is the case in this project. For the purposes of that study, this notion of distinct but internally coherent religious traditions should have died the death of a thousand qualifications. The preface makes many of these qualifications and invites more. Nonetheless, it continues not simply to haunt but to structure the study. That this assumption continues to do so much work in a project as attentive to differences as this one is testifies to its power within the study of religion.

If I am arguing that notions of tradition inappropriately continue to structure too much of our contemporary inquiry, we should also attend to an important recent development that has offered the notion of tradition itself a new lease on life. Over the past two and a half decades, the areas of philosophy of religion and religious ethics have been profoundly influenced by Alasdair MacIntyre's championing of tradition as a model of moral inquiry.[30] MacIntyre argues that rational justification must be understood in relation to particular traditions of inquiry—such as Thomism—not in terms of arguments that are valid for all mature subjects everywhere. Rather than juxtaposing reason and tradition, this model contends that rationality is inseparable from a history of arguments. Tradition, as conceived by MacIntyre, is this history of arguments developing through time—not a fixed set of beliefs and/or practices.[31]

Precisely because MacIntyre's conception of tradition is an account of rational inquiry, it is crucially different from the notion of a religious tradition—such as Buddhism, Christianity, or even Catholicism—that operates in much popular and scholarly discourse on religion. For instance, the tradition MacIntyre champions, Thomism, is both more inclusive and less inclusive than "Catholicism." It is more inclusive because any adequate account of this tradition would have to give Aristotle a major role, even though Aristotle lies outside any conventional usage of the term Catholicism despite wide recognition of his influence on it. Thomism is less inclusive because it excludes, in MacIntyre's account, a great deal—probably the majority—of what most people mean by the term Catholicism. Despite Aquinas's remarkable impact in Catholic thought and life, the Catholic tradition cannot be reduced to Thomism. The most obvious examples might be the kinds of religious practices highlighted by

---

[30] I focus here particularly on his account in Alasdair C. MacIntyre, *Three Rival Versions of Moral Enquiry: Encyclopedia, Genealogy, and Tradition: Being Gifford Lectures Delivered in the University of Edinburgh in 1988* (Notre Dame, IN: University of Notre Dame Press, 1990).

[31] MacIntyre, *Three Rival Versions*, 65. In their attention to histories of inquiry, embodied in communities over time, MacIntyre's traditions entail more than Neville's focus on core texts and motifs.

scholars studying lived religion. Yet it is perhaps more telling that MacIntyre's account of the Thomist tradition effectively excludes a great deal of twentieth-century Catholic thought, specifically "much of the Catholic modernism of the early twentieth century and... fashionable Catholic thought since Vatican II."[32] Thomism is not a synonym for Catholicism, and Catholicism is not a tradition of moral inquiry in the relevant sense. If the case cannot be made with respect to Thomism and Catholicism, it is unlikely to be made for other traditions either.[33] My point in this context is not to critique MacIntyre's account of tradition but to demonstrate that the notion of tradition that he is defending—which is a model of rational inquiry—is crucially different from the notion of discrete "religious traditions" with which we are here concerned.

Of course, one response to these points would be to argue that, if this is the case, then MacIntyre just points to the need to reform the usage of terms such as Catholicism. Perhaps we should redraw the boundaries of "Catholicism" to correspond to the Thomist tradition that MacIntyre identifies. Such a move would seem to be in line with the wishes of some Catholics concerned about the dissolution of a centralized, distinctive, and authoritative tradition. MacIntyre's notion of tradition would thus provide a criterion for distinguishing genuine Catholicism from its semblances. The problems with such a strategy, however, are multiple. Let me suggest two: This way of defining religious traditions is at odds with the goal of understanding the ways that religion functions in people's lives and using the study of religion to understand actual religious actors and communities better. Since many—if not most—individuals who understand themselves to be Catholic do not meaningfully participate in the tradition MacIntyre identifies at Thomism, defining "Catholicism" in these terms leaves huge swaths of the population outside of our inquiry. Defining Catholicism so narrowly fundamentally marginalizes the study of Catholicism.

---

[32] MacIntyre, *Three Rival Versions*, 71.

[33] Notably, MacIntyre does not think that all religions are constituted by traditions of rational inquiry. To the contrary, he is defending tradition against the approaches of other Christians who seek to develop arguments that will be convincing to all rational subjects everywhere. Nonetheless, my point here is that even in what would seem to be the easiest case we cannot make the argument for the tradition of inquiry being a religious tradition.

A second concern is specific to MacIntyre's account of tradition. MacIntyre's notion of tradition is strongest when the boundaries are fuzzy. It is least compelling in relation to the historical evidence when traditions are conceived as clearly bounded systems. As I have argued elsewhere, MacIntyre often draws the boundaries of tradition more definitively and more narrowly than his own leading insights justify. The most valuable aspects of his project, by contrast, are attentive to the ways that traditions are constantly engaging with and incorporating questions, insights, and challenges that initially appeared outside the tradition.[34] To use MacIntyre's account of tradition as a way to define traditions as distinct but coherent entities, then, both builds on the weakest points of his project and draws conclusions unwarranted by the project. Despite the importance of MacIntyre's treatment of tradition, it should not be seen as salvaging, whether intentionally or inadvertently, the notion of distinct religious traditions in the study of religion.

We are left, then, with the possibility of stipulating particular notions of traditions. There will be purposes for which doing so may be entirely appropriate and illuminating, but notions of religions or religious traditions as discrete and coherent entities should have a far less prominent role than they currently do in structuring the study of religion.

PROMISING SIGNS

These limitations to the notion of tradition suggest that we need richer accounts of the sources that inform particular religious groups and actors. A particular individual's or group's relation to earlier instantiations of the religious tradition should be conceived as a question to be probed rather than a presupposition that defines the frame of the inquiry. In this respect, we should recognize that it is a largely empirical question to what degree a particular group's religiosity can be understood or explained in terms of its relation to

---

[34] For instances where MacIntyre treats traditions as bounded systems, see MacIntyre, *Three Rival Versions*, 119–20. I discuss these issues in Thomas A. Lewis, "On the Limits of Narrative: Communities in Pluralistic Society," *Journal of Religion* 86, no. 1 (2006): 55–80.

other instantiations of what we refer to as Buddhism, Judaism, or Hinduism.

We do not simply need more history but a broader history—in which the religious "tradition" functions as only one among several factors informing particular religious individuals, groups, and practices. Although no individual scholar can cover all of the relevant material—the earlier history identified as part of that tradition, the broader intellectual context of the day, the social history of the setting, other traditions circulating at the time, etc.—the religious tradition as such should not always be the dominant frame or the frame that distinguishes work done in religious studies from that done in departments of history or of philosophy. Each of the various contextualizations will illuminate different aspects of the material under study. The scholar of religion should in principle be concerned with each of these rather than defaulting to a projected notion of a coherent "tradition" behind the practices of a particular community, even when—perhaps especially when—the community understands itself in these terms.

Fortunately, important bodies of contemporary work are moving in this direction. Much recent scholarship by historians of religion falls under this category. Attention to the notion of "lived religion" is driven in part by the idea that the majority of most people's actual religious behavior cannot be understood as the application of the teachings or beliefs that are typically taken to define the tradition.[35] Nor will it do to conceptualize this behavior as "popular religion," where this is conceived as a lesser, corrupted form of the tradition proper. Instead, this body of scholarship focuses on practice (variously theorized) and looks beyond elites.[36] The resulting studies avoid presumptions that people do or even could take up pre-established normative beliefs uncritically or mechanically. Such studies expand the use of ethnography and material culture, as well as of non-elite texts. These methods are not unique to the study of religion, but many

---

[35] For some of the defining treatments of this approach, see David D. Hall, ed., *Lived Religion in America: Toward a History of Practice* (Princeton: Princeton University Press, 1997). My discussion draws particularly on the introductory essay by Robert Orsi, "Everyday Miracles: The Study of Lived Religion," 3–21, especially 7–9.

[36] Regarding the strands of practice theory informing treatments of lived religion, see Laurie F. Maffly-Kipp, Leigh Eric Schmidt, and Mark R. Valeri, eds., *Practicing Protestants: Histories of Christian Life in America, 1630–1965* (Baltimore: Johns Hopkins University Press, 2006), especially the introduction.

who quickly see their importance in other contexts may be slower to appreciate their significance in studying religion. Central to this approach is the idea that if we hope to understand the behaviors of most religious actors, we will need to go far beyond—and sometimes leave behind—the kinds of official teachings and "basic facts" that are often taken to constitute religious literacy and that continue to play prominent roles in many of our introductory courses.

Such developments are not limited to the historians in the field. Though quite far from the study of lived religion, work such as Dan Arnold's *Brains, Buddhas, and Believing*, discussed in Chapter 1, demonstrates that work on the early Buddhist thinker Dharmakīrti is crucially illuminated by attending to debates between Dharmakīrti and Hindu interlocutors.[37] Arnold uses the categories of Buddhist and Hindu, but the work they do is carefully circumscribed. As we saw, they function mainly to make the point that these categories do not generate or correspond to the key disagreements in the debate. The references to these religions function as much negatively as positively.

In light of these and other promising examples from diverse sub-fields of the study of religion, one might think that the conception against which I am arguing is no longer a force in the field. There is something to be said for this: the "Introduction to Tradition X" course seems rarer and rarer, for instance, and few scholars of religion define ourselves principally as scholars of entire religions. Nonetheless, the categories continue to do significant work—organizing our undergraduate curricula, our graduate programs, our professional societies (perhaps especially their sections), and our job descriptions.

As we seek to understand particular religious actors, associations, and artifacts, we must situate the object of inquiry not simply in relation to an ostensible religious tradition but also in relation to other contemporaneous intellectual, social, and political developments as well as other relevant traditions (insofar as these can be described as discrete in a given context). Treating the study of religion otherwise is a relic of a view of religion as *sui generis*—as a phenomenon fundamentally distinct from other social phenomena and, in this case, from "other religions." We need not abandon terms such as

[37] Dan Arnold, *Brains, Buddhas, and Believing: The Problem of Intentionality in Classical Buddhist and Cognitive-Scientific Philosophy of Mind* (New York: Columbia University Press, 2012).

Christianity or Buddhism altogether, but we need to recognize, probe, and be attentive to their limits. In doing so, we need to focus on and champion those developments in the field—in our scholarship, in our undergraduate curricula, in our graduate training, and in our structural organization—that move beyond separate traditions as the basic categories structuring work in our field and the understanding of religion more broadly.

To claim that these shifts are relevant not only to advanced developments within the field but also to the broader understanding of religion returns us to the concern with which this chapter began: to respond to the need for a more sophisticated understanding of religion in our public discourse—to contribute to a more informed public engaging religion's ongoing role in the contemporary world. Prothero's work, after all, emerges from the recognition that our public discourse is sorely lacking in the resources to think well about religion. In suggesting that we need to reject approaches such as Prothero's in favor of work with the nuance of Dan Arnold's *Brains, Buddhas, and Believing,* I can be seen as effectively suggesting we abandon any realistic attempt to speak to a broader audience. Or, one might think that what I have put my finger on is not a contrast between basic ways of framing inquiry in our field but rather a much more familiar contrast between work intended for a broad audience beyond the field and the more sophisticated quality of most work in the field. Am I, implicitly, simply once more ruing the oversimplification that comes from moving out of the scholarly tome or advanced seminar and into the public forum?

No. Even if the issues at stake here concern what I take to be some of the leading methodological developments in religious studies as an academic discipline, they are no less important beyond the academy. They concern precisely what we most urgently need for intelligent and skillful engagement in public life. They are not merely abstruse technical points but involve just the kind of thinking about religion that is urgently needed throughout our society. The problem with Prothero's proposal is not that it is just a bit too simple and does not go far enough; it is that it moves us in the wrong direction, telling us to look at the wrong things for understanding religion in the world today. In looking for alternatives, I want to suggest that what we need are not new grand syntheses but more focused studies of groups and developments. Such work need not be so particularistic that it focuses on only one person or one neighborhood. It can attend to a movement or a series of movements, and it may be explicitly comparative across different groups. This work is crucial because it allows us to see what is going on with many of the most widely influential groups in a way that is much more effective and illuminating than just trying to focus on doctrines or simply conceiving their religious claims as ideological cover. It can bring sophistication about the limits of the notion of tradition to bear in work reaching a broader audience. That is essential to making the study of religion integral to the understanding of our contemporary world. And without such thinking, we will face steep hurdles in confronting contemporary social, economic, and political challenges both at home and abroad.

Conclusion

Hegel or Nietzsche?

Collectively, these chapters have proposed a philosophy of religion that self-consciously reflects on and critiques its normative commitments as well as the concepts and categories through which we study religion. It includes students and scholars of a wide range of traditions, scrutinizes its own pasts and present, attends to the conceptualization of religion, and actively engages other subfields of the study of religion. These interventions have sought to elaborate what it means to conceive of philosophy of religion in terms of philosophical analysis of diverse questions and topics generated by the study of particular religious phenomena as well as by the very process of studying religion. Classic questions about the existence of God or the nature of religious language are not left behind, but they are no longer allowed to define the field.

Philosophy of religion conducted along these lines will consist in a conversation of students and scholars specializing in different materials, histories, and historical contexts coming together to exchange about common topics that are themselves conceptualized and reconceptualized through this conversation itself. As suggested in Chapter 4, we should not underestimate the potential of these conversations to alter the participants, to unsettle and subsequently transform the commitments that make them who they are. As the conversation progresses, it will become less deeply marked by the Christian background that shapes so much current work on philosophy of religion. As it does so, it will become a less marginal subfield of religious studies.

This philosophy of religion will engage several audiences beyond itself. At the first level, insofar as it both learns from and adds to broader conversations in the field, religious studies as a whole will be one of its crucial audiences. I have sought to demonstrate the vital role of philosophical analysis in the treatment of topics of broad concern in religious studies. To call for a revitalized philosophy of religion that is integral to religious studies, however, is not to call for domination. It is to view philosophy of religion as one subfield among others of religious studies, not as the unique center of the field. I do not seek a return to an earlier stage in which philosophers of religion dominated our theories and methods seminars. My vision is methodologically pluralistic. This methodological pluralism, particularly when these approaches engage with each other, produces much of the field's strength, depth, and energy.

At a second level, to highlight the study of religion's normativity is, perhaps surprisingly, to illuminate its commonalities with other disciplines. Much of the point of Chapter 2 is to reject claims for the exceptionalism of the study of religion. It belongs in the modern university, not because it is not normative, but because normativity is pervasive—in philosophy, political science, history, and other fields that are seen as central to the academy. The defense of normativity—and the explicit interrogation thereof—is developed in sympathy with those who want to locate the study of religion squarely within the humanities and social sciences. Situated here, religious studies can contribute powerfully to a wide range of interdisciplinary discussions, particularly at a moment when so many across the university find themselves examining religion.

Finally, as Chapter 5 in particular brings out, seemingly abstruse debates in philosophy of religion and religious studies more broadly, about concepts such as how to define a tradition, have tremendous implications beyond the university. In this respect, a third level of our audience is public discourse about religion and connected topics. While we often imagine our disciplinary methodological squabbles to be relevant only to us, today they have substantial implications for global affairs.

This vision has been developed through extensive engagement with recent scholarship as well as, in one chapter, early modern thought. The book as a whole has been centrally concerned with the field's history—both recent and distant. These discussions, however, have been more than a literature review. They have been elaborated, directly and indirectly, in conjunction with normative claims about directions the field ought to take. Thus, while the precise form of the conjunction of history and normativity has varied through the chapters, this nexus—history and normativity—has been a persistent current throughout the book. It is a fitting conclusion to the project, then, to reflect more directly and explicitly on the broader significance of this attention to history and particularly on its relation to normative claims.

Attention to history is by no means unusual in the contemporary academic landscape. Important work in religious ethics has been dedicated to retelling the history of Western ethical thought. Much of the most influential recent scholarship in religious studies has focused on a critical examination of the field's history. Across many disciplines, works informed by Nietzschean and Foucaultian notions of genealogy have developed critical readings of crucial historical junctures. Nonetheless, the degree of explicit reflection on the theoretical presuppositions of engagements with history has varied widely.

Despite the diversity among these developments, the decisive conceptual presuppositions of much prominent work manifesting a turn to history can be traced back to two major figures from the nineteenth century: G. W. F. Hegel and Friedrich Nietzsche. While Hegel has been particularly significant for thinkers such as Charles Taylor, Alasdair MacIntyre, and many pragmatists, Nietzsche's impact—through a notion of genealogy taken up most influentially by Michel Foucault—is even more obvious.[1] Both explicitly and implicitly,

---

[1] Regarding Hegel's significance for Taylor, see the latter's first major tome: Charles Taylor, *Hegel* (Cambridge: Cambridge University Press, 1975). Regarding Hegel's largely unacknowledged presence in MacIntyre, see Richard J. Bernstein, *Philosophical Profiles: Essays in a Pragmatic Mode* (Philadelphia: University of Pennsylvania Press, 1986), especially 138–9, and Thomas A. Lewis, *Religion, Modernity, and Politics in Hegel* (Oxford: Oxford University Press, 2011), 179–202. For examples of the connections to pragmatism, see Jeffrey Stout, *Democracy and Tradition* (Princeton: Princeton University Press, 2004); Jeffrey Stout, "The Spirit of Pragmatism: Bernstein's Variations on Hegelian Themes," *Graduate Faculty Philosophy Journal* 33, no. 1 (2012): 185–246; Jeffrey Stout, "What Is It That Absolute Knowing Knows?," *Journal of Religion* 95, no. 2 (2015): 163–82; Robert Brandom, *Tales of the Mighty Dead: Historical Essays in the Metaphysics of Intentionality* (Cambridge: Harvard University Press, 2002), 178–234; Robert Brandom, *A Spirit of Trust: A Semantic Reading of Hegel's Phenomenology*, 2014, http://www.pitt.edu/~brandom/spirit_of_trust_2014.html; and Robert Stern, *Hegelian Metaphysics* (Oxford: Oxford University Press, 2011). For other important discussions of the significance of history to normative inquiry, see Richard Rorty, J. B. Schneewind,

Nietzschean notions of genealogy have been central to much important scholarship dedicated to revealing the occlusions and uncovering the absences in our histories.

For this reason, we might productively probe the possibilities and significance of turning to history by studying crucial features of the thought of these two figures. Both Hegel and Nietzsche are subject to deeply divergent readings; to avoid triviality, even a brief treatment will need to take a stand on interpretive debates that cannot be fully explored here. My hope is that an account that confines itself to the decisive threads of powerful, even if not fully unpacked, interpretations will place the most important issues in relief. Moreover, beginning with Nietzsche will allow us to consider whether Hegel can account for much that we want to take from Nietzsche. The result, I argue in broad strokes, is a more compelling, Hegelian account of history and normativity. Such a brief discussion will by no means settle the debates, but it will help to illuminate the necessity of engaging our pasts—both distant and recent—in order to chart our futures.

NIETZSCHEAN GENEAOLOGY

Nietzsche's genealogy, most prominently in his *Genealogy of Morals*, writes a history of power and accident. Eschewing history as progress or as decline, genealogy rejects not simply teleology but continuity. While the *Genealogy* can appear as a narrative of decline, its greater challenge lies in the attention to disjunctures, reversals, and unintended consequences. Nietzsche claims to illuminate the pervasiveness of the will to power, to expose the instinctual drives hidden

and Quentin Skinner, eds., *Philosophy in History: Essays in the Historiography of Philosophy* (Cambridge: Cambridge University Press, 1984); Alasdair C. MacIntyre, *Whose Justice? Which Rationality?* (Notre Dame, IN: University of Notre Dame Press, 1988); Alasdair C. MacIntyre, *Three Rival Versions of Moral Enquiry: Encyclopedia, Genealogy, and Tradition: Being Gifford Lectures Delivered in the University of Edinburgh in 1988* (Notre Dame, IN: University of Notre Dame Press, 1990); and Charles Taylor, *Sources of the Self: The Making of the Modern Identity* (Cambridge: Harvard University Press, 1989). On Nietzsche, see Michel Foucault, "Nietzsche, Genealogy, History," in *Language, Counter-Memory, Practice: Selected Essays and Interviews*, ed. D. F. Bouchard (Ithaca: Cornell University Press, 1977), 139–64, and the discussion below.

behind claims about morality, self-sacrifice, and justice. This subterfuge goes all the way down: "We are unknown to ourselves," not simply cleverly deceiving others.[2] Yet neither is this history to be understood simply in terms of contending wills to power. Much of the force of Nietzsche's genealogy lies in the attention to accidents, to the unintended consequences that tumble forth in the wake of other shifts: "it must be obvious which color is a hundred times more vital for a genealogist of morals than blue: namely *gray*."[3] Ambiguities are pervasive; little is vivid. Nietzsche's notion of genealogy thus highlights the significance of the will to power, of accident, and of discontinuity. In doing so, Nietzsche makes the study of history, broadly speaking, significant less because present ideas or practices can be illuminated by their origins or the development of a tradition than because it exposes the frequently hidden operations of power as well as the dramatic shifts often concealed under the veneer of claims of tradition.

To grasp history in these terms is to lessen the significance of origins as well as, more importantly, to distinguish between the origin and the purpose of a practice. The historical beginning of a practice such as punishment may bear no relation to its present purpose:

> purposes and utilities are only *signs* that a will to power has become master of something less powerful and imposed upon it the character of a function; and the entire history of a "thing," an organ, a custom can in this way be a continuous sign-chain of ever new interpretations and adaptations whose causes do not even have to be related to one another but, on the contrary, in some cases succeed and alternate with one another in a purely chance fashion.[4]

Practices of punishment, private ownership, democracy, and so forth over time come to be dominated by different wills to power. The history of democracy, then, appears as a "continuous sign-chain," lending the appearance of sameness to a diverse array of purposes and functions. Justifications of democracy, for instance, that appeal to a purported origin and foundational purpose are nothing more than rationalizations for the power operating through these practices in

---

[2] Friedrich Wilhelm Nietzsche, *On the Genealogy of Morals*, in *Basic Writings of Nietzsche*, trans. and ed. Walter Kaufmann (New York: Modern Library, 2000), Preface:1 [451]. Cited by chapter and section number, with the page from this translation in square brackets.

[3] Nietzsche, *Genealogy of Morals*, Preface:7 [457].

[4] Nietzsche, *Genealogy of Morals*, II:12 [513].

the present. Though driven in each instance by the will to power, this series of successions is not a line of progress or even subject to any overarching rule. Accident plays an ineliminable, unpredictable role.[5]

As profoundly as these elements of Nietzsche's genealogy challenge common ways of thinking about history, ethics, and our own self-understanding, one can make at least modest versions of the above claims without undermining the concepts of ethics or morality. Nietzsche's attentiveness to the subtle operations of power may enable us to see through the self-deceiving justifications that advance and justify oppression. We may better see the oppression concealed within seemingly neutral practices as well as appreciate better the vagaries, inconsistencies, and shifts within history.

More to the point, many contemporary theorists do a great deal of this. Much scholarship on the history of the study of religion attends to the ways in which past scholarship on religion, despite claiming a kind of neutral standpoint, has advanced the interests of colonial and neo-imperial powers. Talal Asad, David Chidester, Timothy Fitzgerald, and Tomoko Masuzawa, for instance, develop genealogies that expose the subtle—and sometimes not so subtle—instances of oppression enabled and justified by prominent modern Western conceptions of religion.[6] Though these recent appeals to genealogy are often mediated by Michel Foucault, the issues are no less pertinent to Nietzsche's genealogy.

Despite their sweeping criticisms, these authors generally abstain from taking on the most radical dimensions of Nietzsche's challenge. They learn from the above elements of Nietzsche's genealogy while remaining in key respects comfortable: employed in this manner, genealogy exposes occlusions, power, and accident yet does not fundamentally challenge the coherence of the very idea of justice or morality. Many contemporary deployments of genealogy seem to be

[5] Michel Foucault is particularly helpful on these points; Foucault, "Nietzsche, Genealogy, History."

[6] Talal Asad, *Genealogies of Religion: Discipline and Reasons of Power in Christianity and Islam* (Baltimore: Johns Hopkins University Press, 1993); Talal Asad, *Formations of the Secular: Christianity, Islam, Modernity* (Stanford, CA: Stanford University Press, 2003). David Chidester, *Savage Systems: Colonialism and Comparative Religion in Southern Africa* (Charlottesville: University Press of Virginia, 1996); Timothy Fitzgerald, *Discourse on Civility and Barbarity: A Critical History of Religion and Related Categories* (Oxford: Oxford University Press, 2007); and Tomoko Masuzawa, *The Invention of World Religions, Or, How European Universalism Was Preserved in the Language of Pluralism* (Chicago: University of Chicago Press, 2005).

developed largely to expose the injustice and oppression entailed by a particular history, without challenging the frequently unarticulated notions of justice, ethics, and truth that motivate the projects in the first place. They are in many respects seeking to set the record straight for the sake of those who have suffered and continue to suffer at the hand of dominant exercises of power.[7]

As praiseworthy as this goal is, precisely this position holds back from what Nietzsche sees as the most radical entailments of his genealogy. The third and final essay of the *Genealogy* takes up the question of where we might find some who have overcome or escaped the ascetic ideal he has been critiquing. After rejecting several other possibilities, Nietzsche turns to those who reject Christianity, which has been so closely connected to this ascetic ideal through much of Western history: "these hard, severe, abstinent, heroic spirits who constitute the honor of our age; all these pale atheists, anti-Christians, immoralists, nihilists."[8] Today's "new atheists," such as Richard Dawkins, Daniel Dennett, and Sam Harris, provide vivid illustrations.

For Nietzsche, even they have not escaped, *"for they still have faith in truth."*[9] This faith in and subordination to truth is one more instantiation—actually "the strictest, most spiritual formulation"—of the ascetic ideal itself:[10]

> Don't come to me with science when I ask for the natural antagonist of the ascetic ideal, when I demand: "where is the opposing will expressing the *opposing ideal?*" Science is not nearly self-reliant enough to be that; it first requires in every respect an ideal of value, a value-creating power, in the *service* of which it could *believe* in itself—it never creates values.[11]

To understand the pursuit of truth as the "will to truth" and therewith as another guise of the will to power is to radically relativize the value of truth.[12] Truth does not frame our investigation of values but is rather one value among others.

---

[7] Whether Foucault himself moves out of this position I take to be beyond the scope of the present piece. Nonetheless, I think we might take his later emphasis on ethics to represent an effort to address these issues.

[8] Nietzsche, *Genealogy of Morals*, III:24 [585].

[9] Nietzsche, *Genealogy of Morals*, III:24 [586].

[10] Nietzsche, *Genealogy of Morals*, III:27 [596].

[11] Nietzsche, *Genealogy of Morals*, III:25 [587].

[12] On these points see Robert B. Pippin, *Modernism as a Philosophical Problem: On the Dissatisfactions of European High Culture*, 2nd edn. (Malden, MA: Blackwell, 1999), 90–6.

Treating truth as a value and therewith relativizing it vis-à-vis other values, Nietzsche renders problematic most appeals to or arguments for any particular values—such as justice—as well as the very conception of what they—justice, morality, etc.—are. Their truth will not save them. The resulting situation has provoked persistent challenges for the interpretation of the text. Nietzsche's relativization of the will to truth—in the sense of a rendering it one will among others—can appear to undermine what has happened up until this point in the work. It certainly calls into question a reading of the first two essays as advocating a straightforward, naturalistic reduction of human action to being merely the result of biologically grounded instincts. Genealogy had seemed to be driven by a more scrupulous respect for the specifics of truth than other models of history, but here Nietzsche seems to tell us that we need not take truth so seriously. In doing so, he appears to many to undermine the coherence of any normative ethical view. Interpreters of Nietzsche have developed substantial arguments for a coherent normative vision coming out of his project. Bernard Reginster, Robert Pippin, and Christopher Janaway offer three important examples, but there are many others.[13] Broadly speaking, I am sympathetic to these attempts to give a reading of Nietzsche that does not fall prey to his own critical engagement with the will to truth. My own view, which I cannot defend here, would attend to Nietzsche's engagement with aesthetics, with Dionysius, and with self-affirmation and would take seriously his critique of the will to truth by not seeking to ground this ethic in claims of truth. To say that I think such a vision can be made coherent, however, is not to say that I advocate it.

Moreover, for the present purposes, developing such an account will not overcome the somewhat peculiar position of scholars such as Asad, Chidester, Fitzgerald, and Masuzawa. For even if we can develop an ethical vision out of Nietzsche's position, it will not be one that salvages the value of truth that still does so much to orient their projects. Nor will it support the general concerns about injustice and oppression that seem no less integral to their work. It will not rebuild these but reject, or at least severely demote, them. And while

---

[13] Bernard Reginster, *The Affirmation of Life: Nietzsche on Overcoming Nihilism* (Cambridge: Harvard University Press, 2006); Pippin, *Modernism as a Philosophical Problem*, 78–113; and Christopher Janaway, *Beyond Selflessness: Reading Nietzsche's Genealogy* (Oxford: Oxford University Press, 2007).

such a strategy might still support an account of how we ought to live—thereby not undermining ethics altogether—it would seem to be at odds with many scholarly projects we value. Nietzsche's genealogy, then, stands at odds with—and poses deep challenges to—many contemporary projects that have drawn heavily on certain elements of his genealogical method. Moreover if my sketch of the implications of Nietzsche's account of the will to truth are on track, this tension is not peculiar to the recent projects I have mentioned: Nietzsche's genealogy ultimately poses profound challenges to the ascetic ideals that he shows are integral to any recognizably scholarly work.

A HEGELIAN ALTERNATIVE

If Nietzsche ultimately threatens—as much as he initially appears to frame—the kinds of historical projects that have prompted this book, then we might reasonably ask how else we can conceptualize these projects as well as the broader turn to history present in this volume. Moreover, can we articulate an account that learns from Nietzsche's attention to the operations of power and the unveiling of occlusions without also undermining the power of these scholarly projects themselves? Here, I want to suggest, Foucault was largely right: Hegel stands waiting for us at the end of the road.[14] Hegel's treatments of history offer resources for conceptualizing the normative significance of history that we cannot forgo. His *Phenomenology of Spirit*, his lectures on the histories of art, religion, and philosophy, and his philosophy of history itself support a compelling conception of history as crucial to understanding where we are and where we ought to go.

To draw upon Hegel for these reasons inevitably generates deep suspicions—and with reason. His accounts of history have often been viewed as the paradigm of triumphalist history written by the victors. Moreover, the way that he tends to locate "others" from his

---

[14] I refer, of course, to Foucault's famous claim that "[w]e have to determine the extent to which our anti-Hegelianism is possibly one of his tricks directed against us, at the end of which he stands, motionless, waiting for us"; Michel Foucault, *The Archaeology of Knowledge*, trans. A. M. Sheridan Smith (New York: Pantheon Books, 1972), 235.

own present—such as contemporary Africans, Asians, Jews, and Catholics—in the past seems closely associated with dire political consequences. For many, then, to turn to Hegel on history is to turn to the most dangerous aspects of his corpus.

An adequate response to these charges requires both identifying the way that these accusations misconstrue crucial elements of Hegel's project and acknowledging the unavoidable dangers entailed by the inevitability of normative judgments. Recent Hegel scholarship has done much to illuminate Hegel in a way that dissipates some of the concerns about totalitarianism, ethnocentrism, and imperialism that have been associated with his thought. This family of "non-traditional" interpretations rejects readings of Hegel as positing a superhuman, cosmic spirit cutting a singular, teleological path across the "slaughter-bench of history" toward the Germanic state.[15] These non-traditional readings are not new in rejecting a totalitarian reading of Hegel's politics; but by rejecting a cosmic monist reading of Hegel's spirit, they more clearly demonstrate a way to articulate and appreciate Hegel's most important contributions to reflections on the normative significance of history while avoiding some of the most problematic positions that have frequently been attributed to him.[16] While these non-traditional readings do not obviate these concerns entirely, they advance the discussion substantially by revealing more clearly what Hegel has to teach us about reason in history as well as distinguishing the specious from the genuine risks of this vision.

Many of the key issues emerge most vividly and succinctly in Hegel's *Phenomenology of Spirit*. Here Hegel develops and executes a conception of rational development that is historically embedded. It traces developments in consciousness and in shapes of spirit by attending closely to the way in which each moment or stage produces immanent contradictions that drive a movement to the next

---

[15] Regarding these developments in the scholarship and the nomenclature of "non-traditional," see James Kreines, "Hegel's Metaphysics: Changing the Debate," *Philosophy Compass* 1, no. 5 (2006): 466–80. On the broader landscape of recent work on Hegel on ethics and religion, see Thomas A. Lewis, "Beyond the Totalitarian: Ethics and the Philosophy of Religion in Recent Hegel Scholarship," *Religion Compass* 2, no. 4 (2008): 556–74.

[16] Critics frequently charge that this interpretive current sanitizes and domesticates Hegel by denying all elements of his thought that are uncomfortable to a purported contemporary philosophical standard. Against this view, I argue that this line of interpretation provides both a better reading of his corpus and a more attractive intellectual position. See Lewis, *Religion, Modernity, and Politics in Hegel.*

moment.[17] In the reading I want to sketch, we can speak of a development as constituting rational progress insofar as it resolves—or at least partially resolves—contradictions that were experienced as immanent within the previous stage. Such contradictions might involve the incompatibility of two deeply held commitments and/or the manner in which a way of life undermines the preconditions necessary to make it viable. While the contradiction is somehow experienced within this standpoint itself, by those inhabiting this standpoint, the source of the tension may not be clearly grasped or comprehended, particularly by those in the midst of the contradiction. Progress is defined not vis-à-vis any sort of yardstick or other standard of judgment external to the process but rather by criteria immanent to the development itself—even if these criteria can only be articulated in retrospect. The project does not apply or impose an external method, procedure or formula. One of Hegel's ways of putting this point is to say that "since consciousness is examining itself, all that remains for us is merely to watch what is going on."[18] Insofar as we are observers of this development, we do not need to impose our standards upon it. Such claims do not entail an attempt to gain access to some purportedly pre-conceptual reality but to focus on the way that movement is generated by contradictions immanent to one stage and that rationality is demonstrated by the way that the next moment overcomes those contradictions.

Perhaps more precisely, the next moment only is the "next" moment in the relevant sense by virtue of its overcoming these contradictions. Only in this manner does it constitute progress rather than simply temporal succession. This point is crucial to avoiding some of the more problematic claims that have often been attributed to Hegel: As much as Hegel links reason and normativity to history, he does not claim that all history is progress. His philosophy of history emphasizes the contrast between a *philosophy* of history and history as such. Where the former traces developments in the consciousness of freedom, history itself—i.e., the aggregate of things that have happened—will include much that does not contribute to these

---

[17] This is not to say either that the *Phenomenology* should be understood as an historical report or that there is not major debate on the nature of the "necessity" of the emergence of the next moment. My language on the latter point is intended to be broad enough to encompass a number of competing interpretations.

[18] G. W. F. Hegel, *Phenomenology of Spirit*, trans. Terry Pinkard, last updated October 30, 2013, http://terrypinkard.weebly.com/phenomenology-of-spirit-page.html, ¶ 85. Cited by paragraph number in the on-line, bilingual edition.

developments.[19] What comes next in history need not, for Hegel, represent actual development; it may not resolve contradictions of previous moments. This point is not glaringly obvious in Hegel's own historical narratives only because his task entails following the threads that do constitute progress. Doing so requires leaving aside the far more numerous instances in which what happened next in a particular time and place did not constitute progress. Contingency plays a role; backsliding happens; progress is not inevitable. The key issue concerns what progress consists in when it occurs, how we give an account of one moment as constituting rational progress vis-à-vis another.

To argue that reason and progress are necessarily measured by standards internal to the development itself would seem to raise concerns about varieties of relativism and skepticism. In broad strokes, the kernel of Hegel's response to this challenge—and a crucial aspect of his project—lies in systematically undermining the coherence of appeals to a standard or criterion external to this history of development itself. Such an appeal or aspiration, Hegel argues, consists in a quest for ghosts that is itself generated by an unjustified conception of a chasm between concept-laden accounts and some imagined "things as they really are" independent of concepts.[20] Over the course of the *Phenomenology* as well as his logic, Hegel seeks to work comprehensively through the variety of ways that such a chasm appears and to demonstrate the fatal inadequacies of each such positing. In other words, Hegel's project consists not in leaping over the limits of pure reason that Kant established but in extending Kant's project by demonstrating that the supposed meaningful object beyond these limits is itself a chimera. Of course, arguing this case is a massive task, and it occupies much of Hegel's corpus. The claims to exhaustiveness, to having precluded all other options, are among his most ambitious objectives. At the same time, it is precisely this aspect of Hegel's project that brings into view the connections to pragmatism.

---

[19] See G. W. F. Hegel, *Vorlesungen über die Philosophie der Weltgeschichte: Band I: Vernunft in der Geschichte*, ed. Johannes Hoffmeister (Hamburg: Felix Meiner Verlag, 1994), 23–49; G. W. F. Hegel, *Lectures on the Philosophy of World History: Introduction: Reason in History*, trans. H. B. Nisbet (Cambridge: Cambridge University Press, 1975), 25–43.

[20] Hegel, *Phenomenology of Spirit*, ¶¶ 73–84. For a particularly helpful secondary account of this point, see Pippin, *Modernism as a Philosophical Problem*, 72.

Beyond these claims about the immanent nature of rational development and the absence of an external criterion for the measurement of this development, however, Hegel also makes *some* kind of claim about completion or closure in his system. Despite the even grander claims that are often attributed to him, this completion or consummation is best understood in terms of the achievement of self-consciousness about this process of development itself. It involves the knowledge that the norms of reason are generated by this process of development, that they have no extra-conceptual grounding, whether in empiricist or transcendent accounts. Achieving this self-consciousness, this transparency regarding the process of development itself, can be described as a kind of "absolute knowing," as Hegel does at the end of the *Phenomenology of Spirit*. Hegel's logic offers a parallel version.[21] Insofar as this completion entails perspective on the process of development itself, this standpoint in some sense involves an elevation above that process; but it does not involve the cessation of learning, knowledge of all finite particulars, or the end of all argument.[22] Such a completion is by no means trivial, but neither should its claims be overstated. It is, in crucial respects, an open-ended consummation.

Grasping Hegel's project in these terms illuminates the essential role of historical accounts in our contemporary constructive work. The justification of our own standpoint, for Hegel, will require a reconstruction of the past that demonstrates the way that those developments we call progress resolve tensions or contradictions that were experienced but could not be overcome from the standpoint of an earlier moment in that history. Attention to history, then, is not optional as we seek to account for our normative commitments. Such a reconstruction or account-giving will not simply be a matter of listing historical events or developments; that would not do the justificatory work. A satisfactory account will have to demonstrate the rationality of each movement or development in terms of the commitments held and the contradictions encountered (and left unresolved) at previous moments. The account thereby gives reasons for judging a new development to constitute rational progress. This is

---

[21] I have developed this point in *Religion, Modernity, and Politics in Hegel*, 89–96, 205–10.

[22] See Pippin, *Modernism as a Philosophical Problem*, 75, and Stout, "What Is It That Absolute Knowing Knows?"

crucial for the turn to history to be more than simply an appeal to the authority of past practice or tradition as such. In this respect Hegel diverges sharply from many forms of conservatism. Authority is not granted to history over reason; rather, a simple juxtaposing of reason and history is itself undermined. The turn to history, then, requires what Hegel considers a philosophical account of history; history as a mere series of events is not justificatory.

Giving such an account requires a fine-grained attention to previous developments. Despite efforts to simplify Hegel into a three-part formula of thesis-antithesis-synthesis, to be imposed on all manner of material, the demands of this approach are much greater. The project can be described in broad strokes, as I have sought to do here; but it can only be carried out through nuanced attention to specifics. Hegel sometimes betrays his own greatest insights by making globalizing claims, yet his project demonstrates its power when working on a smaller scale. Much like Nietzsche's genealogist, Hegelian philosophy "paints its gray in gray"; most of its real work is quite different from grand gestures.[23] Even though Hegel's philosophy of religion played a role in the formation of modern notions of discrete religious traditions, the guiding threads of his project provide resources for resisting such reifying moves—for avoiding the notions of discrete religious traditions critiqued in Chapter 5.

Even more than the others, Chapters 1 and 4 of this book have been carried out in this spirit. The extensive attention to the history of the subfield is intended to constitute something more and other than a literature review. I have sought to provide partial—though always imperfect—justification for the position I am defending by demonstrating how it emerges from the combination of successes and failure of previous moments. I seek to show the view I am defending as a rational way forward in light of where we have been and are. Blanket portrayals cannot accomplish this; much turns on the details.

---

[23] G. W. F. Hegel, *Grundlinien der Philosophie des Rechts*, ed. Eva Moldenhauer and Karl Markus Michel, vol. 7, Werke (Frankfurt am Main: Suhrkamp, 1970), 28; G. W. F. Hegel, *Elements of the Philosophy of Right*, trans. H. B. Nisbet, ed. Allen Wood (Cambridge: Cambridge University Press, 1991), 23. I have drawn attention to the problems Hegel unnecessarily brings upon himself by making grander claims than he needs to—particularly regarding notions of discrete religious traditions—in Thomas A. Lewis, "Hegel's Determinate Religion Today: Foreign yet Not So Far Away," in *Der Begriff der Religion und die Vielfalt der Religionen: Schleiermacher—Hegel—Schelling*, ed. Friedrich Hermanni, Friedrike Schick, and Burkhard Nonnenmacher, Collegium Metaphysicum (Tübingen: Mohr Siebeck, forthcoming 2015).

To link rational justification to giving an account of how we have arrived where we are need not function to sanctify our present commitments whatever they may be. Insofar as we are incapable of constructing a narrative of the way that these commitments overcome contradictions immanent to previous moments, we call our commitments into question. Insofar as we make explicit the contradictions of the present, we call our commitments into question. More significantly, to examine how we have come to think as we do *raises* the question whether we should think as we do; it does not *preclude* the question. And our ability to construct such an account—which demonstrates the rationality of our present standpoint vis-à-vis conflicts of the past— by no means precludes the emergence of tensions within our present views and commitments. This Hegelian account of understanding our own standpoint in relation to the history that has produced it does not automatically justify whatever commitments we happen to hold. Rather, it tells us what a convincing justification will require.

If a more adequate reading of Hegel disarms some of the most persistent criticisms of his thought, we can now return to one of the issues that has made Nietzschean genealogy so attractive in recent years: whether or not we accept Nietzsche's view of the will to truth as a contingent possibility, as the most recent and perhaps final development out of Christianity itself, we can learn much from his attention to the operations of power. Asad, Mahmood, Masuzawa, and others demonstrate how productive this focus can be. Yet nothing in the Hegelian account we have been considering precludes this attention to power. To probe how this Hegelian version of a turn to history contributes to scrutinizing the operations of power, we need to ask precisely how the former understands or conceives the latter kind of work. Can the analysis of power be more than a sideline to the Hegelian approach to history that we are sketching here?

Hegel's analysis of the ways that social practices and institutions mold subjects generates a penetrating perspective for analyzing the kinds of phenomena that genealogists have examined under the rubric of power. We see this in part in Hegel's account of what deeply social creatures we are. We are not most fundamentally animals motivated by a fixed set of basic desires or instincts (though Hegel does not exclude such language altogether). Our most significant and dominant motives are themselves shaped through complex conglomerations of social practices. Moreover, these motives, drives, and desires are often opaque to the subjects themselves. Hegel's emphasis on self-consciousness by no means entails that we are always transparent to ourselves. Many of the commitments that are most authoritative for us and that are pervasively manifest in our social practices will be, at a reflective level, unknown or only vaguely grasped by us. In many cases, such motives and commitments become conscious, even if only partially, when they come into conflict with other motives and commitments. Hegel interprets Sophocles' *Antigone* as a grand portrayal of just such a conflict, one that only becomes apparent when circumstances bring two commitments, each of which is integral to the social world, into direct and irresolvable conflict. Similarly, in *The Philosophy of Right*, the explicit principle of civil society is the individual actor pursuing the satisfaction of his or her own needs and interests. Yet a hidden principle is no less important: the satisfaction of the individual's own ends depends in part on others. This interdependence results in the transformation of my desires, their schooling such that what I desire tends to come into line with others'.[24] Here as well, Hegel shows his ability to identify the hidden effects of social practices and thus to illuminate the pervasive yet almost unnoticed transformations wrought by social practices of which the participants are only obscurely aware.

In other words, an approach that turns to history in part to understand how our present has and has not overcome the tensions in previous moments in our collective history can and should be attentive to hidden forces, subtle effects, and unintended consequences that figure so prominently in Nietzschean genealogies. Moreover, it can attend to these features without undermining the normative ground on which it stands. It can, if successful, critique these operations of power while also offering an account that justifies its own normative validity vis-à-vis other options. Doing so will require, at a minimum, identifying conflicts within the practices being critiqued. It will build on such conflicts to demonstrate the contradictions internal to the standpoint being critiqued. To be sure, this is a tremendously ambitious agenda. I believe it can only ever be partially accomplished. Some of Hegel's own greatest problems derive from claims to be more comprehensive than is possible. Nonetheless, a strategy following these broad outlines seems to offer the greatest prospects for simultaneously acknowledging the historical situatedness of our own standpoint, exposing the hidden

---

[24] Hegel, *Philosophy of Right*, §§ 182–4.

operations of power, and providing a rational justification for our own normative commitments.

Understood along these lines, a Hegelian approach to the significance of history avoids many of the imperialistic and totalitarian implications that are often attributed to his project. Nonetheless, to acknowledge the significance of history in this manner requires us to acknowledge the particularity of our own historical situation. Hegel justifies our judging from that standpoint—not because of some intrinsic superiority but, in part, because it is the only standpoint we have. It is not fixed; we will and should transform. But it is where we stand now. Concretely, this means that the categories on which we presently draw to understand others as well as ourselves will be those emerging from our history, whoever we happen to be. As discussed in Chapter 4, for many in the academic study of religion in North America and Europe today, the particular histories that have shaped these concepts are largely, though by no means exclusively, those of the North Atlantic world.

To respond to this limitation, we need to acknowledge the dangers, the tremendous consequences that have resulted from the deployment of many of "our" concepts in a global context. But that should not lead us to avoid judging, for that strategy results in paralysis and/ or self-deception. Rather, we need to actively pursue, articulate, and critique the contradictions in our own commitments and practices. Encounters with others will play a vital role in this process. And we need to remain open to revising our views—to the realization that our own commitments contain contradictions, some of which will become more apparent in time. Holding normative commitments should not be confused with an unwillingness to revise them. While accepting the ongoing need for future revisions to our views, however, we must also accept the inevitability of our judging others. As alarming as we may initially find Hegel's efforts to demonstrate the superiority of his own view to all others of which he is aware, holding any view inevitably entails something of just this sort: holding it to be superior to any alternatives of which one is aware.[25] Such judgments bring risks, but such risks are ones we cannot avoid. Rather than attempting to avoid or deny them, we need to face them as self-consciously and reflectively as we can. Only then can we hope to avoid their most dangerous forms.

---

[25] I have developed a version of this point in Lewis, "Hegel's Determinate Religion Today."

Bibliography

Armour, Ellen T. "Theology in Modernity's Wake." *Journal of the American Academy of Religion* 74, no. 1 (2006): 7–15.

Arnal, William. "The Collection and Synthesis of 'Tradition' and the Second-Century Invention of Christianity." *Method and Theory in the Study of Religion* 23 (2011): 193–215.

Arnold, Dan. *Brains, Buddhas, and Believing: The Problem of Intentionality in Classical Buddhist and Cognitive-Scientific Philosophy of Mind.* New York: Columbia University Press, 2012.

Asad, Talal. *Genealogies of Religion: Discipline and Reasons of Power in Christianity and Islam.* Baltimore: Johns Hopkins University Press, 1993.

Asad, Talal. *Formations of the Secular: Christianity, Islam, Modernity.* Stanford: Stanford University Press, 2003.

Asad, Talal. "Thinking about Religion, Belief, and Politics." In Orsi, *The Cambridge Companion to Religious Studies*, 17–35.

Badiou, Alain. *Saint Paul: The Foundation of Universalism.* Translated by Ray Brassier. Stanford: Stanford University Press, 2003.

Bagger, Matthew C. *The Uses of Paradox: Religion, Self-Transformation, and the Absurd.* New York: Columbia University Press, 2007.

Bell, Catherine M. *Ritual Theory, Ritual Practice.* Oxford: Oxford University Press, 1992.

Berkson, Mark A. "Conceptions of Self/No-Self and Modes of Connection: Comparative Soteriological Structures in Classical Chinese Thought." *Journal of Religious Ethics* 33, no. 2 (2005): 293–331.

Bernstein, Richard J. *Philosophical Profiles: Essays in a Pragmatic Mode.* Philadelphia: University of Pennsylvania Press, 1986.

Brandom, Robert. *Tales of the Mighty Dead: Historical Essays in the Metaphysics of Intentionality.* Cambridge: Harvard University Press, 2002.

Brandom, Robert. *Between Saying and Doing: Towards an Analytic Pragmatism.* Oxford: Oxford University Press, 2008.

Brandom, Robert. *A Spirit of Trust: A Semantic Reading of Hegel's Phenomenology*, 2014, http://www.pitt.edu/~brandom/spirit_of_trust_2014.html.

Bucar, Elizabeth M. "Methodological Invention as a Constructive Project: Exploring the Production of Ethical Knowledge through the Interaction of Discursive Logics." *Journal of Religious Ethics* 36, no. 3 (2008): 355–73.

Bucar, Elizabeth M. *Creative Conformity: The Feminist Politics of U.S. Catholic and Iranian Shi'i Women.* Washington, DC: Georgetown University Press, 2011.

Bucar, Elizabeth M., Grace Y. Kao, and Irene Oh. "Sexing Comparative Ethics: Bringing Forth Feminist and Gendered Perspectives." *Journal of Religious Ethics* 38, no. 4 (2010): 654–9.

Bucar, Elizabeth M., and Aaron Stalnaker, eds. *Religious Ethics in a Time of Globalism*. New York: Palgrave Macmillan, 2012.

Bush, Stephen S. *Visions of Religion: Experience, Meaning and Power*. Oxford: Oxford University Press, 2014.

Chidester, David. *Savage Systems: Colonialism and Comparative Religion in Southern Africa*. Charlottesville: University Press of Virginia, 1996.

Clairmont, David A. *Moral Struggle and Religious Ethics: On the Person as Classic in Comparative Theological Contexts*. Malden, MA: Wiley-Blackwell, 2011.

Crisp, Oliver D., and Michael C. Rea, eds. *Analytic Theology: New Essays in the Philosophy of Theology*. Oxford: Oxford University Press, 2009.

Croce, Benedetto. *What Is Living and What Is Dead of the Philosophy of Hegel*. Translated by Douglas Ainslie. London: Macmillan, 1915.

Dancy, Jonathan, ed. *Normativity*. Oxford: Blackwell Publishers, 2000.

Davis, G. Scott. "Two Neglected Classics of Comparative Ethics." *Journal of Religious Ethics* 36, no. 3 (2008): 375–403.

Davis, G. Scott. *Believing and Acting: The Pragmatic Turn in Comparative Religion and Ethics*. Oxford: Oxford University Press, 2012.

De Vries, Hent. *Philosophy and the Turn to Religion*. Baltimore: Johns Hopkins University Press, 1999.

De Vries, Hent. "Introduction: Why Still 'Religion'?" In de Vries, *Religion: Beyond a Concept*, 1–98.

De Vries, Hent, ed. *Religion: Beyond a Concept*. New York: Fordham University Press, 2008.

Decosimo, David. "Comparison and the Ubiquity of Resemblance." *Journal of the American Academy of Religion* 78, no. 1 (2010): 226–58.

Dole, Andrew. "Schleiermacher and Otto on Religion." *Religious Studies* 40, no. 4 (2004): 389–413.

Dole, Andrew. *Schleiermacher on Religion and the Natural Order*. Oxford: Oxford University Press, 2010.

Dole, Andrew, and Andrew Chignell, eds. *God and the Ethics of Belief: New Essays in Philosophy of Religion*. Cambridge: Cambridge University Press, 2005.

Dubuisson, Daniel. *The Western Construction of Religion: Myths, Knowledge, and Ideology*. Translated by William Sayers. Baltimore: Johns Hopkins University Press, 2003.

Eck, Diana L. *A New Religious America: How a "Christian Country" Has Now Become the World's Most Religiously Diverse Nation*. San Francisco: HarperSanFrancisco, 2001.

Farneth, Molly. "Hegel's Sacramental Politics: Confession, Forgiveness, and Absolute Spirit." *Journal of Religion* 95, no. 2 (2015): 183–97.

Firestone, Chris L., and Nathan Jacobs. *In Defense of Kant's Religion*. Bloomington: Indiana University Press, 2008.

Firestone, Chris L., and Stephen R. Palmquist, eds. *Kant and the New Philosophy of Religion*. Bloomington: Indiana University Press, 2006.

Fitzgerald, Timothy. *The Ideology of Religious Studies*. Oxford: Oxford University Press, 2000.

Fitzgerald, Timothy. *Discourse on Civility and Barbarity: A Critical History of Religion and Related Categories*. Oxford: Oxford University Press, 2007.

Flew, Antony, and Alasdair C. MacIntyre, eds. *New Essays in Philosophical Theology*. New York: Macmillan, 1955.

Flood, Gavin. "Reflections on Tradition and Inquiry in the Study of Religions." *Journal of the American Academy of Religion* 74, no. 1 (2006): 47–58.

Foucault, Michel. *The Archaeology of Knowledge*. Translated by A. M. Sheridan Smith. 1st American edn. New York: Pantheon Books, 1972.

Foucault, Michel. "Nietzsche, Genealogy, History." In *Language, Counter-Memory, Practice: Selected Essays and Interviews*, edited by D. F. Bouchard, 139–64. Ithaca: Cornell University Press, 1977.

Frankenberry, Nancy K., ed. *Radical Interpretation in Religion*. Cambridge: Cambridge University Press, 2002.

Furey, Constance M. "Body, Society, and Subjectivity in Religious Studies." *Journal of the American Academy of Religion* 80, no. 1 (2012): 7–33.

Godlove, Jr., Terry F. "Saving Belief: On the New Materialism in Religious Studies." In Frankenberry, *Radical Interpretation in Religion*, 10–24.

Goodchild, Philip. "Continental Philosophy of Religion: An Introduction." In Goodchild, *Rethinking Philosophy of Religion*, 1–39.

Goodchild, Philip, ed. *Rethinking Philosophy of Religion: Approaches from Continental Philosophy*. New York: Fordham University Press, 2002.

Green, Ronald Michael. *Religious Reason: The Rational and Moral Basis of Religious Belief*. Oxford: Oxford University Press, 1978.

Green, Ronald Michael. *Religion and Moral Reason: A New Method for Comparative Study*. Oxford: Oxford University Press, 1988.

Hall, David D., ed. *Lived Religion in America: Toward a History of Practice*. Princeton: Princeton University Press, 1997.

Hammerschlag, Sarah. *The Figural Jew: Politics and Identity in Postwar French Thought*. Chicago: University of Chicago Press, 2010.

Hare, John. *The Moral Gap*. Oxford: Clarendon Press, 1996.

Hasker, William. "Analytic Philosophy of Religion." In *The Oxford Handbook of Philosophy of Religion*, edited by William J. Wainwright, 421–46. Oxford Handbooks in Philosophy. Oxford: Oxford University Press, 2005.

Hegel, Georg Wilhelm Friedrich. *Grundlinien der Philosophie des Rechts*. Vol. 7. Werke. Frankfurt am Main: Suhrkamp, 1970.

Hegel, Georg Wilhelm Friedrich. *Lectures on the Philosophy of World History: Introduction: Reason in History*. Translated by H. B. Nisbet. Cambridge: Cambridge University Press, 1975.

Hegel, Georg Wilhelm Friedrich. *Vorlesungen über die Philosophie der Religion*. Edited by Walter Jaeschke. 3 vols. Hamburg: Felix Meiner Verlag, 1983–85.

Hegel, Georg Wilhelm Friedrich. *Lectures on the Philosophy of Religion*. Translated by R. F. Brown, P. C. Hodgson, and J. M. Stewart. 3 vols. Berkeley: University of California Press, 1984–87.

Hegel, Georg Wilhelm Friedrich. *Elements of the Philosophy of Right*. Translated by H. B. Nisbet. Edited by Allen Wood. Cambridge: Cambridge University Press, 1991.

Hegel, Georg Wilhelm Friedrich. *Die Vernunft in der Geschichte*. Vol. 1 of *Vorlesungen über die Philosophie der Weltgeschichte*. Edited by Johannes Hoffmeister. 6th edn. Hamburg: Felix Meiner Verlag, 1994.

Hegel, Georg Wilhelm Friedrich. *Hegel's Philosophy of Mind*. Translated by W. Wallace, A. V. Miller, and M. J. Inwood. Oxford: Clarendon Press, 2007.

Hegel, Georg Wilhelm Friedrich. *Lectures on the Philosophy of Spirit 1827–8*. Translated by Robert R. Williams. Oxford: Oxford University Press, 2007.

Hegel, Georg Wilhelm Friedrich. *Phenomenology of Spirit*. Translated by Terry Pinkard. Last updated October 30, 2013, http://terrypinkard. weebly.com/phenomenology-of-spirit-page.html.

Heim, Maria. "Buddhist Ethics: A Review Essay." *Journal of Religious Ethics* 39, no. 3 (2011): 571–84.

Herdt, Jennifer A. "Religious Ethics, History, and the Rise of Modern Moral Philosophy: Focus Introduction." *Journal of Religious Ethics* 28, no. 2 (2000): 165–88.

Herdt, Jennifer A. *Putting on Virtue: The Legacy of the Splendid Vices*. Chicago: University of Chicago Press, 2008.

Hollywood, Amy M. *Sensible Ecstasy: Mysticism, Sexual Difference, and the Demands of History*. Chicago: University of Chicago Press, 2002.

James, William. *The Varieties of Religious Experience*. Cambridge: Harvard University Press, 1985.

Janaway, Christopher. *Beyond Selflessness: Reading Nietzsche's Genealogy*. Oxford: Oxford University Press, 2007.

Kahn, Jonathon S. *Divine Discontent: The Religious Imagination of W. E. B. Du Bois*. Oxford: Oxford University Press, 2009.

Kant, Immanuel. *Groundwork of the Metaphysics of Morals*. In *Practical Philosophy*, edited by Mary J. Gregor, translated by Mary J. Gregor and Allen W. Wood, 37–108. The Cambridge Edition of the Works of Immanuel Kant. Cambridge: Cambridge University Press, 1999.

Kelsay, John. *Arguing the Just War in Islam*. Cambridge: Harvard University Press, 2007.

Kelsay, John. "Just War, Jihad, and the Study of Comparative Ethics." *Ethics & International Affairs* 24, no. 3 (2010): 227–38.

Kelsay, John. "Response to Papers for 'Ethnography, Anthropology, and Comparative Religious Ethics' Focus." *Journal of Religious Ethics* 38, no. 3 (2010): 485–93.

Kelsay, John. "The Present State of the Comparative Study of Religious Ethics." *Journal of Religious Ethics* 40, no. 4 (2012): 583–602.

King, Richard. *Orientalism and Religion: Postcolonial Theory, India and "the Mystic East."* London: Routledge, 1999.

Kippenberg, Hans G. *Discovering Religious History in the Modern Age.* Translated by Barbara Harshav. Princeton: Princeton University Press, 2002.

Korsgaard, Christine M. *The Sources of Normativity.* Cambridge: Cambridge University Press, 1996.

Kreines, James. "Hegel's Metaphysics: Changing the Debate." *Philosophy Compass* 1, no. 5 (2006): 466–80.

Lee, Jung H. "The Rhetoric of Context." *Journal of Religious Ethics* 41, no. 4 (2013): 555–84.

Lewis, Thomas A. "Frames of Comparison: Anthropology and Inheriting Traditional Practices." *Journal of Religious Ethics* 33, no. 2 (2005): 225–53.

Lewis, Thomas A. *Freedom and Tradition in Hegel: Reconsidering Anthropology, Ethics, and Religion.* Notre Dame, IN: University of Notre Dame Press, 2005.

Lewis, Thomas A. "On the Limits of Narrative: Communities in Pluralistic Society." *Journal of Religion* 86, no. 1 (2006): 55–80.

Lewis, Thomas A. "Beyond the Totalitarian: Ethics and the Philosophy of Religion in Recent Hegel Scholarship." *Religion Compass* 2, no. 4 (2008): 556–74.

Lewis, Thomas A. "Ethnography, Anthropology, and Comparative Religious Ethics: Or Ethnography and the Comparative Religious Ethics Local." *Journal of Religious Ethics* 38, no. 3 (2010): 395–403.

Lewis, Thomas A. *Religion, Modernity, and Politics in Hegel.* Oxford: Oxford University Press, 2011.

Lewis, Thomas A. "Vergleichende Ethik in Nordamerika: Methodologische Probleme und Ansätze [expanded and updated]." In *Wertetraditionen und Wertekonflikte: Ethik in Zeiten der Globalisierung,* edited by Gabriele Münnix, 321–35. Nordhausen: Verlag Traugott Bautz, 2013.

Lewis, Thomas A. "Hegel's Determinate Religion Today: Foreign yet Not So Far Away." In *Der Begriff der Religion und die Vielfalt der Religionen: Schleiermacher—Hegel—Schelling,* edited by Friedrich Hermanni, Friedrike Schick, and Burkhard Nonnenmacher. Collegium Metaphysicum Tübingen: Mohr Siebeck, forthcoming 2015.

Lewis, Thomas A., Jonathan W. Schofer, Aaron Stalnaker, and Mark A. Berkson. "Anthropos and Ethics: Categories of Inquiry and Procedures of Comparison." *Journal of Religious Ethics* 33, no. 2 (2005): 177–85.

Lincoln, Bruce. *Holy Terrors: Thinking about Religion after September 11.* 2nd edn. Chicago: University of Chicago Press, 2006.

Little, David, and Sumner B. Twiss. *Comparative Religious Ethics: A New Approach.* San Francisco: Harper & Row, 1978.

Lovin, Robin W., and Frank Reynolds. "In the Beginning." In Lovin and Reynolds, *Cosmogony and Ethical Order*, 1–35.

Lovin, Robin W., and Frank Reynolds, eds. *Cosmogony and Ethical Order: New Studies in Comparative Ethics.* Chicago: University of Chicago Press, 1985.

McCutcheon, Russell T. *Critics Not Caretakers: Redescribing the Public Study of Religion.* Albany: State University of New York Press, 2001.

MacIntyre, Alasdair C. *After Virtue: A Study in Moral Theory.* 2nd edn. Notre Dame, IN: University of Notre Dame Press, 1984.

MacIntyre, Alasdair C. *Whose Justice? Which Rationality?* Notre Dame, IN: University of Notre Dame Press, 1988.

MacIntyre, Alasdair C. *Three Rival Versions of Moral Enquiry: Encyclopedia, Genealogy, and Tradition: Being Gifford Lectures Delivered in the University of Edinburgh in 1988.* Notre Dame, IN: University of Notre Dame Press, 1990.

Maffly-Kipp, Laurie F., Leigh Eric Schmidt, and Mark R. Valeri, eds. *Practicing Protestants: Histories of Christian Life in America, 1630–1965.* Baltimore: Johns Hopkins University Press, 2006.

Mahmood, Saba. *Politics of Piety: The Islamic Revival and the Feminist Subject.* Princeton: Princeton University Press, 2005.

Mann, William, ed. *The Blackwell Guide to the Philosophy of Religion.* Malden, MA: Blackwell, 2005.

Martin, Dale B., and Patricia Cox Miller, eds. *The Cultural Turn in Late Ancient Studies: Gender, Asceticism, and Historiography.* Durham: Duke University Press, 2005.

Masuzawa, Tomoko. *The Invention of World Religions, Or, How European Universalism Was Preserved in the Language of Pluralism.* Chicago: University of Chicago Press, 2005.

Miller, Richard B. "On Making a Cultural Turn in Religious Ethics." *Journal of Religious Ethics* 33, no. 3 (2005): 409–43.

Neville, Robert C. "Preface." In Neville, *The Human Condition*, xv–xxvi.

Neville, Robert C., ed. *The Human Condition.* The Comparative Religious Ideas Project. Albany: State University of New York Press, 2001.

Neville, Robert C., ed. *Religious Truth.* The Comparative Religious Ideas Project. Albany: State University of New York Press, 2001.

Neville, Robert C., ed. *Ultimate Realities.* The Comparative Religious Ideas Project. Albany: State University of New York Press, 2001.

Nietzsche, Friedrich Wilhelm. *On the Genealogy of Morals.* In *Basic Writings of Nietzsche*, translated by Walter Arnold Kaufmann, 449–607. New York: Modern Library, 2000.

Nussbaum, Martha C. "Non-Relative Virtues: An Aristotelian Approach." In Nussbaum and Sen, *The Quality of Life*, 242–69.

Nussbaum, Martha C. *Women and Human Development: The Capabilities Approach.* Cambridge: Cambridge University Press, 2000.

Nussbaum, Martha C., and Amartya K. Sen, eds. *The Quality of Life.* Oxford: Clarendon Press, 1993.

Oh, Irene. *The Rights of God: Islam, Human Rights, and Comparative Ethics.* Washington, DC: Georgetown University Press, 2007.

Orsi, Robert A. *Thank You, St. Jude: Women's Devotion to the Patron Saint of Hopeless Causes.* New Haven: Yale University Press, 1996.

Orsi, Robert A. "Everyday Miracles: The Study of Lived Religion." In Hall, *Lived Religion in America*, 3–21.

Orsi, Robert A. *Between Heaven and Earth: The Religious Worlds People Make and the Scholars Who Study Them.* Princeton: Princeton University Press, 2005.

Orsi, Robert A., ed. *The Cambridge Companion to Religious Studies.* Cambridge: Cambridge University Press, 2011.

Otto, Rudolf. *The Idea of the Holy: An Inquiry into the Non-Rational Factor in the Idea of the Divine and Its Relation to the Rational.* Translated by John W. Harvey. 2nd edn. Oxford: Oxford University Press, 1958.

Phillips, D. Z., and Timothy Tessin, eds. *Philosophy of Religion in the 21st Century.* Basingstoke: Palgrave, 2001.

Pippin, Robert B. *Modernism as a Philosophical Problem: On the Dissatisfactions of European High Culture.* 2nd edn. Malden, MA: Blackwell, 1999.

Prothero, Stephen. *Religious Literacy: What Every American Needs to Know—and Doesn't.* San Francisco: HarperOne, 2008.

Prothero, Stephen. *God Is Not One: The Eight Rival Religions That Run the World—and Why Their Differences Matter.* New York: HarperOne, 2010.

Proudfoot, Wayne. *Religious Experience.* Berkeley: University of California Press, 1985.

Putnam, Hilary. "Objectivity and the Science-Ethics Distinction." In Nussbaum and Sen, *The Quality of Life*, 143–57.

Rapp, Jennifer R. "A Poetics of Comparison: Euripides, Zhuangzi, and the Human Poise of Imaginative Construction." *Journal of the American Academy of Religion* 78, no. 1 (2010): 163–201.

Rea, Michael C. "Introduction." In Crisp and Rea, *Analytic Theology*, 1–30.

Reginster, Bernard. *The Affirmation of Life: Nietzsche on Overcoming Nihilism.* Cambridge: Harvard University Press, 2006.

Reynolds, Frank, and David Tracy, eds. *Myth and Philosophy.* Albany: State University of New York Press, 1990.

Reynolds, Frank, and David Tracy, eds. *Discourse and Practice.* Albany: State University of New York Press, 1992.

Reynolds, Frank, and David Tracy, eds. *Religion and Practical Reason: New Essays in the Comparative Philosophy of Religions*. Albany: State University of New York Press, 1994.

Roberts, Tyler T. *Encountering Religion: Responsibility and Criticism after Secularism*. New York: Columbia University Press, 2013.

Rorty, Richard. "The Historiography of Philosophy: Four Genres." In Rorty, Schneewind, and Skinner, *Philosophy in History*, 49–75.

Rorty, Richard. "Religion as a Conversation-Stopper." In *Philosophy and Social Hope*, 168–74. London: Penguin Books, 1999.

Rorty, Richard. "Religion in the Public Square: A Reconsideration." *Journal of Religious Ethics* 31, no. 1 (2003): 141–9.

Rorty, Richard, J. B. Schneewind, and Quentin Skinner, eds. *Philosophy in History: Essays in the Historiography of Philosophy*. Cambridge: Cambridge University Press, 1984.

Schellenberg, J. L. *Prolegomena to a Philosophy of Religion*. Ithaca: Cornell University Press, 2005.

Schilbrack, Kevin. *Philosophy and the Study of Religions: A Manifesto*. Malden, MA: Wiley Blackwell, 2014.

Schleiermacher, Friedrich. *On Religion: Speeches to Its Cultured Despisers*. Translated by Richard Crouter. 2nd edn. Cambridge: Cambridge University Press, 1996.

Schleiermacher, Friedrich. *The Christian Faith*. Translated by James S. Stewart and H. R. Mackintosh. Edinburgh: T&T Clark, 1999.

Schneewind, J. B. *The Invention of Autonomy: A History of Modern Moral Philosophy*. Cambridge: Cambridge University Press, 1998.

Schofer, Jonathan W. *The Making of a Sage: A Study in Rabbinic Ethics*. Madison: University of Wisconsin Press, 2005.

Schofer, Jonathan W. "Self, Subject, and Chosen Subjection: Rabbinic Ethics and Comparative Possibilities." *Journal of Religious Ethics* 33, no. 2 (2005): 255–91.

Schofer, Jonathan W. "Embodiment and Virtue in a Comparative Perspective." *Journal of Religious Ethics* 35, no. 4 (2007): 715–28.

Schofer, Jonathan W. *Confronting Vulnerability: The Body and the Divine in Rabbinic Ethics*. Chicago: University of Chicago Press, 2010.

Schopen, Gregory. *Bones, Stones, and Buddhist Monks: Collected Papers on the Archaeology, Epigraphy, and Texts of Monastic Buddhism in India*. Honolulu: University of Hawai'i Press, 1997.

Schopen, Gregory. *Buddhist Monks and Business Matters: Still More Papers on Monastic Buddhism in India*. Honolulu: University of Hawai'i Press, 2004.

Schweiker, William. "Responsibility and Comparative Ethics." In *Power, Value, and Conviction: Theological Ethics in the Postmodern Age*, 111–34. Cleveland: Pilgrim Press, 1998.

Slingerland, Edward. "Who's Afraid of Reductionism? The Study of Religion in the Age of Cognitive Science." *Journal of the American Academy of Religion* 76, no. 2 (2008): 375–411.

Smith, Jonathan Z. "In Comparison a Magic Dwells." In Smith, *Imagining Religion*, 19–35.

Smith, Jonathan Z. *Imagining Religion: From Babylon to Jonestown*. Chicago: University of Chicago Press, 1982.

Smith, Jonathan Z. *Drudgery Divine: On the Comparison of Early Christianities and the Religions of Late Antiquity*. Chicago: University of Chicago Press, 1990.

Smith, Jonathan Z. "Religion, Religions, Religious." In Taylor, Mark C., *Critical Terms for Religious Studies*, 269–84.

Smith, Jonathan Z. *Relating Religion: Essays in the Study of Religion*. Chicago: University of Chicago Press, 2004.

Sockness, Brent W. *Against False Apologetics: Wilhelm Hermann and Ernst Troeltsch in Conflict*. Tübingen: Mohr Siebeck, 1998.

Stalnaker, Aaron. "Comparative Religious Ethics and the Problem of 'Human Nature.'" *Journal of Religious Ethics* 33, no. 2 (2005): 187–224.

Stalnaker, Aaron. *Overcoming Our Evil: Human Nature and Spiritual Exercises in Xunzi and Augustine*. Washington, DC: Georgetown University Press, 2006.

Stalnaker, Aaron. "Virtue as Mastery in Early Confucianism." *Journal of Religious Ethics* 38, no. 3 (2010): 404–28.

Stern, Robert. *Hegelian Metaphysics*. Oxford: Oxford University Press, 2011.

Stout, Jeffrey. "Weber's Progeny, Once Removed." *Religious Studies Review* 6, no. 4 (1980): 289–95.

Stout, Jeffrey. *Ethics after Babel: The Languages of Morals and Their Discontents*. 1st Princeton edn. Princeton: Princeton University Press, 2001.

Stout, Jeffrey. *Democracy and Tradition*. Princeton: Princeton University Press, 2004.

Stout, Jeffrey. "The Spirit of Pragmatism: Bernstein's Variations on Hegelian Themes." *Graduate Faculty Philosophy Journal* 33, no. 1 (2012): 185–246.

Stout, Jeffrey. "What Is It That Absolute Knowing Knows?" *The Journal of Religion* 95, no. 2 (2015): 163–82.

Swinburne, Richard. "The Probability of the Resurrection." In Dole and Chignell, *God and the Ethics of Belief*, 117–30.

Taliaferro, Charles. "Philosophy of Religion." In *The Stanford Encyclopedia of Philosophy*, edited by Edward N. Zalta, 2011, http://plato.stanford.edu/archives/spr2011/entries/philosophy-religion/.

Taylor, Charles. *Hegel*. Cambridge: Cambridge University Press, 1975.

Taylor, Charles. "Philosophy and Its History." In Rorty, Schneewind, and Skinner, *Philosophy in History*, 17–30.

Taylor, Charles. *Sources of the Self: The Making of the Modern Identity*. Cambridge: Harvard University Press, 1989.

Taylor, Charles. "Comparison, History, Truth." In Reynolds and Tracy, *Myth and Philosophy*, 37–55.

Taylor, Mark C., ed. *Critical Terms for Religious Studies*. Chicago: University of Chicago Press, 1998.

Tracy, David. *The Analogical Imagination: Christian Theology and the Culture of Pluralism*. New York: Crossroad, 1981.

Tracy, David. "On the Origins of the Philosophy of Religion: The Need for a New Narrative of Its Founding." In Reynolds and Tracy, *Myth and Philosophy*, 11–36.

Trakakis, Nick. *The End of Philosophy of Religion*. London: Continuum, 2008.

Tweed, Thomas A. *Crossing and Dwelling: A Theory of Religion*. Cambridge: Harvard University Press, 2006.

Twiss, Sumner B. "Four Paradigms in Teaching Comparative Religious Ethics." In *Explorations in Global Ethics: Comparative Religious Ethics and Interreligious Dialogue*, edited by Sumner B. Twiss and Bruce Grelle, 11–33. Boulder, CO: Westview Press, 1998.

Twiss, Sumner B. "Comparison in Religious Ethics." In *Blackwell Companion to Religious Ethics*, edited by William Schweiker, 147–55. Malden, MA: Blackwell, 2005.

Twiss, Sumner B., and Bruce Grelle. "Human Rights and Comparative Religious Ethics: A New Venue." *The Annual of the Society of Christian Ethics* 23 (1995): 21–48.

Vásquez, Manuel A. *More than Belief: A Materialist Theory of Religion*. Oxford: Oxford University Press, 2011.

Wedgwood, Ralph. *The Nature of Normativity*. Oxford: Clarendon Press, 2007.

Wildman, Wesley. *Religious Philosophy as Multidisciplinary Comparative Inquiry: Envisioning a Future for the Philosophy of Religion*. Albany: State University of New York Press, 2010.

Wolterstorff, Nicholas. *Inquiring about God: Selected Essays, Vol. 1*. Edited by Terence Cuneo. Cambridge: Cambridge University Press, 2010.

Wolterstorff, Nicholas. *Practices of Beliefs: Selected Essays, Vol. 2*. Edited by Terence Cuneo. Cambridge: Cambridge University Press, 2010.

Wood, Allen W. *Hegel's Ethical Thought*. Cambridge: Cambridge University Press, 1990.

Yearley, Lee H. *Mencius and Aquinas: Theories of Virtue and Conceptions of Courage*. Albany: State University of New York Press, 1990.

Yearley, Lee H. "Ethics of Bewilderment." *Journal of Religious Ethics* 38, no. 3 (2010): 436–60.

Zagzebski, Linda Trinkaus. *Philosophy of Religion: An Historical Introduction*. Malden, MA: Blackwell, 2007.

Index

Printed and bound by CPI Group (UK) Ltd, Croydon, CR0 4YY